In Focus: The Case for Privatising the BBC

D1512877

This publication is based on research that forms part of
the Paragon Initiative.

This five-year project will provide a fundamental reassessment
of what government should – and should not – do. It will put
every area of government activity under the microscope and
analyse the failure of current policies.

The project will put forward clear and considered solutions to
the UK's problems. It will also identify the areas of government
activity that can be put back into the hands of individuals,
families, civil society, local government, charities and markets.

The Paragon Initiative will create a blueprint for a better,
freer Britain – and provide a clear vision of a new relationship
between the state and society.

IN FOCUS:
THE CASE FOR PRIVATISING THE BBC

EDITED BY PHILIP BOOTH

with contributions from

RYAN BOURNE

TIM CONGDON

STEPHEN DAVIES

CENTO VELJANOVSKI

Institute of
Economic Affairs

First published in Great Britain in 2016 by
The Institute of Economic Affairs
2 Lord North Street
Westminster
London SW1P 3LB
in association with London Publishing Partnership Ltd
www.londonpublishingpartnership.co.uk

The mission of the Institute of Economic Affairs is to improve understanding of the
fundamental institutions of a free society by analysing and expounding the role of
markets in solving economic and social problems.

A CIP catalogue record for this book is available from the British Library.

ISBN 978-0-255-36725-7

Many IEA publications are translated into languages other
than English or are reprinted. Permission to translate or to reprint
should be sought from the Director General at the address above.

Typeset in Kepler by T&T Productions Ltd
www.tandtproductions.com

Printed and bound in Great Britain by Hobbs the Printers Ltd

CONTENTS

THE AUTHORS

Philip Booth

Philip Booth is Academic and Research Director at the Institute of Economic Affairs (IEA) and Professor of Finance, Public Policy and Ethics at St Mary's University, Twickenham. He was formerly Professor of Insurance and Risk Management at the Cass Business School, where he also served as Associate Dean. He has an undergraduate degree in economics from the University of Durham and a PhD in finance. He is a Fellow of the Institute of Actuaries and of the Royal Statistical Society. Previously, Philip Booth worked for the Bank of England as an adviser on financial stability issues. He has written widely, including a number of books, on investment, finance, social insurance and pensions, as well as on the relationship between Catholic social teaching and economics.

Ryan Bourne

Ryan Bourne is Head of Public Policy at the IEA and a weekly columnist for *City AM*. He has previously worked at both the Centre for Policy Studies and Frontier Economics, and has written widely on a range of economic issues. He has both MA (Cantab) and MPhil qualifications in economics from the University of Cambridge.

Tim Congdon

Tim Congdon is often regarded as the UK's leading 'monetarist' economist, and was one of the foremost advocates of so-called

Thatcherite monetarism in the late 1970s and early 1980s. He is currently a professor of economics at the University of Buckingham, where he has established a new research institute, the Institute of International Monetary Research (www.mv-pt.org). His books include *Money in a Free Society* (New York: Encounter Books, 2011).

Stephen Davies

Stephen Davies is Head of Education at the IEA. From 1979 until 2009 he was Senior Lecturer in the Department of History and Economic History at Manchester Metropolitan University. He has also been a Visiting Scholar at the Social Philosophy and Policy Center at Bowling Green State University in Bowling Green, Ohio, and Program Officer at the Institute for Humane Studies at George Mason University in Virginia.

Cento Veljanovski

Cento Veljanovski is Managing Partner of Case Associates, and IEA Fellow in Law and Economics. He was previously Research and Editorial Director at the IEA (1989–91), and held academic positions at University College London (1984–87), Oxford University (1974–84) and other UK, North American and Australian universities. He holds several degrees in law and economics (BEc, MEc, DPhil). He has written many books and articles on media and broadcasting, industrial economics, and law and economics, including *Selling the State: Privatisation in Britain* (Weidenfeld: 1988) and, for the IEA, *Freedom in Broadcasting* (1988), *The Economics of Law* (1990; second edition, 2006) and, together with Cambridge University Press, *Economic Principles of Law* (2007).

FOREWORD

One of the central questions of our age is how our society, the economy and the state cope with the changes brought about by technological progress and disruptive new companies. While firms such as Uber, Amazon and Airbnb have radically changed how their industries operate – generally in favour of the consumer and to the detriment of existing, often heavily regulated, producers – the British Broadcasting Corporation (BBC) continues to use a funding model first devised in the 1920s to compel – through threat of arrest and criminal conviction – the payment of a hypothecated tax to fund its activities.

Although the BBC funding model has remained largely unchanged, the white heat of technology has seen the rest of the industry move on. Content – whether live, recorded or streamed through the Internet – can now be accessed on a variety of devices at almost any time. It is now accessed at a time and in a method convenient to the viewer, not to the television network or the advertiser.

In the light of these changes the question of the future viability of the BBC is of major concern to both economists and politicians.

The authors in this monograph make a persuasive argument that the licence fee is no longer the right way to raise revenue for the BBC. While there was a case for this model when the only way to watch the BBC was through the ownership of a television, and there was no way to prevent anyone who owned a television from watching the BBC, technological developments have demolished this argument. Millennials consume more and more of their broadcast media through a tablet, computer or phone.

Yet, non-payment of the licence fee now accounts for 10 per cent of all criminal convictions in the UK, so we may soon be in the invidious position where a majority of young people watch BBC programmes through devices that are not taxed, while older people who own a television but watch only ITV or Sky Sports are taxed and, in the case of non-compliance, subject to arrest.

Those who support the continuation of the licence fee often do so using two arguments: that the BBC is vital for producing what has become known as 'public service broadcasting', and that the BBC produces news that is non-partisan together with unbiased coverage of current affairs.

Cento Veljanovski, in his chapter, directly engages with the argument that public service broadcasting requires state input, arguing first that the sheer amount of content now available – from the Discovery Channel to religious channels – means that there is vanishingly little broadcasting that the state needs to support and, at the very least, there should be radical changes to how it is supported. Indeed, Veljanovski finds most of the modern justifications for public service broadcasting wanting.

The other authors echo this view and go as far as saying that the whole case for public sector broadcasting has disappeared. With the declining credibility of public good or merit good arguments, more tenuous arguments have been made by supporters of the BBC – mostly based around market failure. But these arguments are largely spurious, the authors claim.

Meanwhile, the monograph also looks at the claim that the BBC is unbiased. Considering that the BBC is responsible for more than 75 per cent of news content in Britain, any question over the impartiality of a state organisation which is such a dominant player should be a major cause for concern.

Considering the constant march of technology, the model of the BBC will need to change – whether politicians wish it to or not. The final chapter comes out in favour of full privatisation so that the BBC will have the freedom to use its undoubted excellence to open a new chapter in its history in which it will be able to take advantage of all the changes in technology as well as the globalisation of the industry.

This monograph – by authors who are experts in their fields - provides a timely and relevant discussion of public service broadcasting and the future of the BBC. It is a blueprint for how the BBC could be freed from the shackles of the state to become a major player on the world media stage. It deserves close attention from those with an interest in the BBC and broadcasting.

MARK LITTLEWOOD
Director General and Ralph Harris Fellow
Institute of Economic Affairs
March 2016

The views expressed in this monograph are, as in all IEA publications, those of the author and not those of the Institute (which has no corporate view), its managing trustees, Academic Advisory Council members or senior staff. With some exceptions, such as with the publication of lectures, all IEA monographs are blind peer-reviewed by at least two academics or researchers who are experts in the field.

ACKNOWLEDGEMENT

The chapter by Tim Congdon is summarised from the ebook *Privatise the BBC* (2014), published by *Standpoint*, London, UK, and also uses material from articles published by the author in *Standpoint*. The IEA is grateful to *Standpoint* for permission to adapt and republish.

SUMMARY

- In the past, the use of a compulsory levy on television sets (a licence fee) to finance the BBC could be justified given the problem of spectrum scarcity and the fact that television signals were a public good (i.e. there was effectively a zero marginal cost of an additional user receiving the signal and no effective mechanism of exclusion). Furthermore, the fact that television sets were bulky, and had no practical use other than watching television programmes, made the collection and enforcement of the licence fee practically viable.

- In recent years, these justifications for the licence fee have evaporated. It is technically straightforward to exclude non-payers from receiving television signals and spectrum scarcity is no longer a practical problem. Furthermore, there is no clear relationship between owning a television set and watching 'television' programmes. Programmes can be watched on computers, phones and tablets; and televisions are used for activities other than watching programmes. The BBC – and to a more limited extent other independent groups and economists – have tried, increasingly desperately, to find other justifications for retaining the licence fee.

- Other models of state funding for so-called public service broadcasting can be justified. For example, there could be a household levy (as in Germany), which could finance a state broadcaster. In a pluralistic society, an alternative would be to have state funding available on a competitive basis to a range of broadcasters and programme producers. This latter proposal has been described as 'an Arts Council for the air'. However, all such mechanisms are prone to capture by interest groups.

- A further problematic feature of the BBC is bias. All institutions exhibit bias – whether consciously or unconsciously. However, the BBC has a worldwide reputation, is funded on a compulsory basis and provides 75 per cent of all televised news. When an institution with such power exhibits bias, this is a far more serious problem.

- There are different types of bias. For example, 'bias by presentation' is illustrated by the description of the 2014 Budget by a BBC journalist as 'back to the land of *Road to Wigan Pier*'. 'Bias by selection' is illustrated by negative portrayals of business outnumbering positive portrayals by a factor of more than eight to one on Radio 4's *Thought for the Day*.

- There are no feasible reforms that can eliminate bias. Instead, the state should uncouple itself from the BBC and remove compulsory sources of funding. Commercial and non-commercial news media can then compete together as they do in print and online media: for example, the *Guardian* is one of the most successful online journalism sources while being supported by a charitable trust.

- There are various ways in which the BBC could be made independent of the state and/or of compulsory funding. Models that have been proposed involve the use of subscription (with the BBC remaining state owned) or allowing the BBC to become a membership organisation (like the National Trust).

- However, there are strong arguments for privatisation on a commercial basis. In the era of *The Sopranos* and *The Man in the High Castle* it can no longer be convincingly argued that commercialisation necessarily leads to dumbing down. Furthermore, membership organisations and mutuals have notoriously poor corporate governance outcomes.

- A further reason for this model of privatisation is that the BBC will struggle to thrive without commercial freedoms. Already only 20 per cent of UK broadcasting revenue comes from public funds and the BBC is, in fact, small compared with international commercial broadcasters. The international potential of a commercialised BBC is such that, one day, its worldwide audiences might be a hundred times as large as its UK audiences. Tying an organisation with such international reach to the UK government and to a compulsory licence fee would stifle it.
- The BBC is not the only broadcaster with a strong relationship with the state. Channel 4 is state owned, though financed by advertising. This is an anachronism and it should be privatised.

TABLES, FIGURES AND BOXES

1 INTRODUCTION: BROADCASTING IN THE TWENTY-FIRST CENTURY

Philip Booth and Stephen Davies

For the past few decades, the British public has been regaled at regular intervals by a pantomime that returns to the stage of public debate when the time for renewal of the BBC's charter comes around. We are told by one side that the licence fee should be abolished, and by the other side that to do so would destroy a great national institution. Meanwhile, the government of the day invariably uses the opportunity this presents to apply not-so-gentle pressure on the BBC's senior management, while the BBC itself tacks and trims to ensure that it gets the best deal possible. All this may soon be a thing of the past. This is not because of a decisive victory for one side or the other in the debate, or because of a popular resistance to payment (although there is such resistance, and it is widespread). Rather, it is because of a technological transformation that is rapidly making the entire debate moot: technology is changing the way that television in particular is made and above all consumed. This means that the licence fee is doomed and will have to be replaced, regardless of what people say or want.

The origins of the licence fee

The question of how to fund television and radio broadcasts arose almost as soon as the technology to make them became available. From an economist's point of view, broadcast radio and television programmes fall into the category of collective goods because they have the quality of non-rivalrous consumption. Having an additional person watch or listen to a broadcast does not impair the initial viewer or listener's consumption of the good. In theory, broadcasting also had the quality of excludability, and so could have been provided as a club good, whereby the service was provided to people in return for a subscription. The problem was that the technology to realise this kind of model was not originally available. This meant that broadcasting fell into the category of a public good, one that is both non-rivalrous in consumption and has non-excludability. In most countries, one of two solutions was adopted. The first solution was to provide radio and later television broadcasting as a pure public good, funded out of general taxation. The problem, of course, was that this had the potential to make broadcasting into an instrument of state propaganda. The second solution was to tie the public goods of radio and television broadcasting to the private good of advertising.

In Britain, however, a third route was adopted. Defenders of the licence fee sometimes present this as a matter of farsighted design, but, in fact, it happened by accident. When radio receivers first became available after Marconi's pioneering experiments, the Post Office was given a power to issue and charge for licences for radio receivers. This was partly a measure intended to control and regulate access, but it was also seen from the start as a revenue-raising device (at that time, the Post Office was one of the principal sources of government revenue). In 1922, manufacturers of radio receivers, along with the Post Office, created the British Broadcasting Company. This was initially funded by the sale of receivers but, as these became more common, the problems of non-rivalrous and non-excludable consumption also emerged – once a certain number of people had a receiver, there was much less incentive for others to also buy one, as they could listen to a broadcast on someone else's set without paying. The Post Office continued to charge for radio licences, and in 1927 the British Broadcasting Company became the British Broadcasting Corporation (BBC), with the Post Office handing over almost all the licence fee income to it. So, the funding of broadcasting by a system of licensing was stumbled upon through the hypothecation of what had been originally just another source of government revenue.

The evolution to a hypothecated television tax

This system, created in the 1920s, made the reception of broadcasts into a kind of club good, which combined a club system of payment by subscription with a monopoly single charge that went to one provider, even when (as after 1955) there were other providers. The system became consolidated and took on its present format in 1946 with the introduction of combined television and radio licences (separate radio-only licences continued to be sold until 1971). The crucial fact that made this feasible was that television broadcasts could only be received via a specific piece of equipment, the television set. That meant that excludability could be created by tying the ownership of the set to a charge that was then used to fund the broadcasts of the BBC (Briggs 1985). However, importantly, though it would have been technically feasible, it was not permitted to buy a piece of equipment that only received ITV programmes (not funded by the licence) and not pay a licence fee. If any television signals were received, the licence had to be bought. This meant that the licence fee was effectively a hypothecated tax (though it was not paid by people who wished to receive no television services whatsoever).

An enforcement mechanism was, of course, required, but this was feasible. The fact that a household is receiving signals can be detected. Furthermore, until recently, television sets were bulky and not easily portable, which meant that the charge for having a set could easily be linked to a specific address. The advent of portable televisions did not really affect this because their reception quality was often so poor that they never caught on as a common platform for watching programming. This meant that the fee became a tax on any household that had the means to receive television broadcasts.

The final piece of the technological jigsaw was that television receivers only had one use – that of receiving television and (sometimes) radio broadcasts. Consequently, anyone who owned one could be assumed to be using it to watch broadcast programming, and this prevented ambiguity. In later years, it became possible to claim that a set was only being used to watch purchased video recordings, but this was uncommon.

There was, of course, a problem of non-compliance. This was dealt with by making failure to pay the fee a criminal rather than a civil offence, and then prosecuting and heavily fining enough evaders to create a deterrent effect. Over time, the number of non-payers increased and reached the point where 10 per cent of all criminal prosecutions were for non-payment of the licence fee (Pirie 2015; Gentleman 2014).

The collapse of the justification for licence fee funding

All this has changed, and the combination of technological facts that made the licensing of receivers a practical way to fund broadcasting no longer exists. The first and fundamental change is that there is now a multiplicity of platforms or devices on which anyone can watch television programmes. You can watch them on laptops, tablets, e-readers and mobile phones. According to a recently released survey in the United States (US) by the Consumer Electronics Association (CEA), these are rapidly becoming the main platforms for television viewers among the so-called millennials (13- to 34-year-olds). Among this group, only

55 per cent reported using conventional televisions as their primary platform for watching television broadcasts, and the trend is clearly for this to become a minority pursuit (CEA 08/01/2015; see also Plunkett 2014).

The response of many at the BBC and elsewhere has been to argue that the majority of television viewing is still done in the traditional way by watching broadcast programmes on conventional television sets. However, the crucial fact is the trend identified in the CEA report and elsewhere. For example, the number of US households that receive television programming only via aerial (6 per cent) will soon be overtaken by those that receive it only via the Internet (currently 5 per cent). In other findings, in 2014, 46 per cent of US television-user households watched video on either a laptop, notebook or netbook (up from 38 per cent in 2013); 43 per cent watched video on a smartphone (up from 33 per cent in 2013); 35 per cent watched video on a tablet (up from 26 per cent in 2013); and 34 per cent watched video on a desktop computer (up from 30 per cent in 2013) (CEA 2014).

A very important point is that these devices are multifunctional – watching television streaming is only one of the many functions they can perform. Consequently, you can reasonably own one for many reasons other than receiving television programmes. In addition, they are typically highly portable; the survey showed that, for consumers, this is their most valuable quality when it comes to watching and listening to media of various kinds. Portability is the way of the future, it would seem. Just as the advent of the small and portable transistor radio destroyed the original radio licence, so portable devices such as mobile telephones, tablets and laptops look set to fatally undermine the television licence. On the one hand, it is extremely difficult to charge something akin to a television licence fee for a mobile phone (and also unjust if it is not used to watch television content). On the other hand, the charging of a licence fee for televisions (assuming it remains possible to define what a television is) might prevent that technology from evolving – there is, essentially, a tax incentive to use phones to watch television rather than use televisions to make phone calls.

What this means, of course, is that people can now watch television anywhere and, crucially, without having to buy a television receiver. This drastically weakens or even breaks the link between having a particular kind of device (which could be linked to an address) and watching television, which was the key to funding the broadcasts through a licence fee for the ownership of the device. Legally, people still need a television licence to watch programmes if they are watched as they are broadcast, regardless of the device used. The problem, of course, is that this is almost impossible to enforce, precisely because the devices in question are used for so many other purposes.

It might be possible to extend the principle of the licence fee and have a 'viewing charge' built in to the cost of every mobile phone, laptop, computer, e-reader and tablet. However, this does not seem likely simply because it would be extremely unpopular, and because it would be very difficult to assign such a charge to the BBC without expensive and complex administration. Any attempt to do this would also lead to many devices being purchased elsewhere in the European Union (EU), and this could not be stopped without breaching EU rules.

Television broadcasts are not a public good

Moreover, ever-larger amounts of television are being either recorded and watched later or viewed through streaming channels such as Netflix. According to very recent surveys, a majority of television content is now watched done on Netflix and other streaming sites (XStream 2015). Most watchers no longer watch shows as they come out; instead, they wait until the shows are available on Netflix or its rivals, and then watch them in large, advertisement-free chunks (Hearn 2015). A report from Nomura revealed that in the US year-on-year viewing figures over the three major networks declined by 12.7 per cent (Roetgers 2015). This is a catastrophic drop and reveals a fundamental shift in the way that television programming is being consumed. Among other things, this is leading, in turn, to profound changes in both viewing habits and the nature and content of programmes (Rainey 2015).

This has devastating implications for the commercial-advertising-funded model of television, as is now being widely pointed out (Wolk 2015). However, it also means that the fallback response to the growth in the range of platforms described above does not work. If people claim (probably truthfully) that they only watch television on their tablet or mobile device via their Netflix subscription, then, even according to the letter of the law, they cannot be charged the licence fee for use of the device in this way. The combination of the two developments of portable, multi-use platforms and delayed consumption of programmes via streaming sites means that the established model is simply blown out of the water.

Of course, the streaming services, together with satellite broadcasters such as Sky, demonstrate a further point. Broadcasting services are now 'excludable'. Compulsory finance for a product can be justified for a 'public' good where it is not possible to exclude non-payers. It is far more difficult to justify compulsory finance for 'club' goods where it is possible to exclude from consumption those who do not pay. Subscription is a more justifiable model for club goods.

Indeed, Netflix is now moving into the production side of the business. This will inevitably crowd out traditional production processes, whether funded by advertising or the licence fee. Instead, the funding will come primarily from a subscription charge. This is part of a wider revolution in the production of television, driven by the sharp decline in production costs and the appearance of dedicated channels and platforms such as YouTube and specialist niche channels based on that model. Much of the content that viewers consume will no longer be produced or (more importantly) delivered by large integrated networks such as the BBC (or, for that matter, ITV or Channel 4). So, the argument that some kind of secured income such as the licence fee is necessary to produce what consumers would like to have loses much of its force.

The licence fee debate should be dead – at least among economists

What all this means is that the whole repetitious argument about whether the television licence fee should be replaced is moot. While academics, politicians and journalists have debated these issues, a technological revolution has completely changed the landscape. In the future, it seems almost certain that the television set will cease to exist as a distinct kind of device, as it will come to be combined with other kinds of devices and platforms such as home computers. Many people will simply not have a conventional television set and will watch television shows on their mobile phone or laptop. They will not watch programmes in the way we have become used to, and the content will increasingly be produced and delivered by organisations very different from the networks and stations of the past, including the BBC. Indeed, it may no longer be meaningful to talk about 'television'. This diverse range of broadcasting provision needs a diverse range of funding sources, with some providers relying on different sources from others.

What might replace the licence fee model of funding the BBC?

The current line of defence is to say that, although the government has not stipulated that households must purchase a TV licence if they have any device capable of being used to watch television, people must still pay the fee if they use such a device to watch a programme at the time it is broadcast, even if they do not own a television set. This leads to situations such as students who are away from home at a student residence being asked to pay a licence fee if they have a laptop. This is both very difficult to enforce and, more importantly, impossible to enforce with any kind of consistency. This will undermine the legitimacy of the entire charge (to the extent that it still has any for many people). Imposing a charge on every single device at the point of sale would be subject to legal challenge from those claiming that they had no intention of using their device to watch television, and it would be highly unpopular.

One solution, which has been floated by the Select Committee on Culture, Media and Sport, is to move to the German model of a flat-rate charge levied on every single household and used only to fund a public broadcaster (Parliamentary Papers 2015). The Director General of the BBC, Tony Hall, has already supported this idea. However, there are serious and principled objections to this. It would effectively be a hypothecated household poll tax and, undoubtedly, would be extremely unpopular politically. Given that, the temptation for one party to pledge its abolition would be ultimately irresistible. This approach would also bring government even closer to the BBC and make the Corporation even more susceptible to political pressure than it is already.

The idea that was popular for many years on the free-market side – that is, switching the BBC to an advertising funded model – is also past its use-by date. The changes described above will radically undermine the entire advertising-based model of broadcasting, which will go the way of advertising-funded print media (rapidly downhill). It is possible that advertising-funded programming may survive in one form or another. However, it is not a viable, stable, long-term model to provide all the funding for a broadcasting organisation.

The solution that economic analysis should now lead us to is as follows. We should recognise that, with changes in technology, television broadcasting has clearly and definitively moved into the club good sector. Both individual programmes and channels can be encrypted and made excludable. This means that the appropriate, and sustainable way of funding it is by a club type subscription method or simple pay-per-view. One or the other of these will be more appropriate for particular kinds of programming. For example, sports broadcasting would rely on a mixture of the two, while serials would rely almost entirely on subscriptions. It is worth pointing out that radio is much less affected and can easily continue to be funded primarily by advertising.

However, this does not really resolve the policy issues – except that it can be concluded that there is no place for the licence fee in the financing of broadcasting: technology has put paid to that. The more general question is what should be the role of government in broadcasting? How should we deal with the ownership of the BBC and Channel 4? And how should so-called public service broadcasting (PSB) be financed? These are the topics that the other authors cover in this book.

Public service broadcasting

In the next chapter, Cento Veljanovski specifically examines PSB. He looks at a number of options for financing it. The first is government subsidy of PSB, available to all broadcasters on a competitive basis. As noted above, this is often known as the 'arts council for the air' option. This has some merit. It would allow, for example, Sky Sports to receive grants for covering minority sports or para-athletics, if they were not commercially viable; Classic FM could apply for grants to broadcast a broader range of classical music that might not have wide audience appeal; Channel 5 might apply for a grant to run a series of science documentaries; and so on. There would be diversity, competition and, hopefully, efficiency in the way resources were used.

If this approach were taken, it would expose the BBC to the full rigours of competition. It would have to find its financing from a mix of grants, subscriptions, commercial rights sales and advertising. If others achieved the objectives of PSB more effectively, they would get the government money.

The view of the authors of this introduction is that this is not the way to go. There is a danger of political capture of the grant-giving body; and the lines of accountability of the quango would not be clear.

But Veljanovski raises a more fundamental question. How do we define 'PSB' in anything like an objective way? The old public good argument for state-financed broadcasting is dead. Those who support some form of compulsory funding for the BBC hold on to more and more tenuous arguments based around what economists term 'market failure'. It is argued that in a free market certain types of content will not be provided that may have benefits to wider society – for example, help create social cohesion or promote education. In other words, they may give rise to externalities. Of course, this is true with a wide range of activities (reading, for example).

Yet the reality of today's multimedia world is an extraordinary multiplicity of channels, programming and other content. It does not appear that there are large unserved markets. It may be the case that people do not watch as much educational content as others think desirable, but this cannot be solved by simply subsidising the creation of more such content. The Discovery Channel, Quest, Yesterday and EWTN, amongst many other conventional channels (some free-to-air, others available cheaply by subscription) and a whole host of on-demand video platforms, show the kind of material that most people would classify as PSB in the sense of having 'positive externalities' or some kind of educational value. If people 'under-consume' such programming, in the current technological age, it is difficult to see how their consumption patterns can be 'corrected'. There is no lack of production of programmes with what might be described as public service characteristics.

Furthermore, broadcasting is just one of many ways in which people try to educate themselves. Perhaps a better model would be for existing private and public funding bodies and other organisations to pursue their missions through broadcasting. This happens to some extent already: the BBC partnered with the Open University to produce the series fronted by Stephanie Flanders on the economists Keynes, Marx and Hayek, for example. The Royal Society, the Arts Council, the Royal Society of Arts (or even the IEA, the Templeton Foundation or the Fabian Society) could commission programming where it is thought that their mission could be promoted in such a way. Perhaps the existence of the BBC crowds out such initiatives and prevents such lateral thinking.

It seems likely that the whole notion of PSB has died in the multichannel world. The arguments for it are tenuous and they do not, anymore, specifically relate to broadcasting.

This takes us on to the institutions. In a world where it has no ring-fenced guaranteed funding and there is no special place for PSB, what should be the future of the BBC as an institution? Before answering that question, we need to consider one of the problems of the BBC that perhaps should make the reform of its ownership a higher priority than it is currently.

Bias and the BBC

Ryan Bourne looks at the empirical evidence on BBC bias. He notes that the BBC is a highly trusted source of news and other information. However, he provides compelling evidence that there is bias in the presentation of news. It is impossible to analyse bias objectively – indeed, Bourne argues that all organisations are subject to biases, and that, of course, includes organisations that assess the bias of other organisations. It is also very difficult to go beyond a case study approach to bias, and such an approach has obvious limitations.

Despite those limitations, there is a very strong case for the BBC to answer. For example, there is considerable evidence of 'bias by omission', which relates to the choice of people who comment on particular news stories and how particular stories are framed and presented. One example of this was on 19 September 2013. The BBC website ran a 'Viewpoints' piece highlighting different opinions on the new policy of taxpayer-funded school meals for all five-to-seven year olds. The government's own pilot study found no health benefits for the policy and did not assess the opportunity cost of the spending. Yet the views promoted on the BBC website included only those who were happy with the policy, together with those who felt that it did not go far enough. It was only when this was pointed out to the BBC that they added alternative views. This is quite different from the coverage of the story in the print media: both the *Guardian* and the *Daily Mail* had balanced accounts. It clearly did not occur to the BBC, until it was pointed out, that it was possible to object to the policy except on the grounds that the government was not spending enough on the initiative.

In addition, there is 'bias by selection' – both of topics and people who present topics. Ryan Bourne comments that there have been many more TV and radio shows dedicated to the subject of inequality on the BBC than, for example, the promotion of economic growth. This is despite the fact that inequality does not rank as a greater concern among the public, and despite the recent fall in conventional measures of inequality. Within some of these inequality shows, there was a clear bias in the selection of guests towards those who considered income and wealth inequality an extremely important and worrying topic. In a similar vein, the BBC Radio 4 *Today* programme has a regular slot called *Thought for the Day*, in which prominent individuals are selected to comment on issues in the news from a religious perspective. Analysis of the content of *Thought for the Day* is striking. In the 167 editions analysed in new research commissioned for Ryan Bourne's chapter, negative comments on business within the slot outweighed positive commentary on business by a factor of more than eight to one.

And, finally, there is 'bias by presentation', which relates to how journalists present stories. One example of this is the way in which BBC journalist Norman Smith covered the 2014 Autumn Statement, reporting that the Office for Budget Responsibility (OBR) had forecast that spending levels as a proportion of gross domestic product (GDP) would be likely to fall to levels last seen in the late 1930s. Rather than just outlining this fact (though that, in itself, would have been a misrepresentation for the reasons mentioned below), the presentation of the story by Smith entailed substantial value judgements about what this would mean:

> when you sit down and read the Office for Budget Responsibility report it reads like a book of doom. It is utterly terrifying, suggesting that spending will have to be hacked back to the levels of the 1930s as a proportion of GDP. That is an extraordinary concept, you're back to the land of *Road to Wigan Pier*.

The journalist could have said that spending as a proportion of national income would be reduced to Australian or Swiss levels. He could have commented on the large differences between the national income definitions used and the different types of spending in the 1930s, which would have shown the projections in a completely different light. He could also have mentioned that spending as a proportion of national income would be very close to 2002 levels. Instead, the journalist chose to represent the budget projections in a particular way.

The BBC's presentation of tax avoidance is also interesting. There has been a proliferation of stories about avoidance, often involving large companies such as Amazon, Starbucks and Google. In 24 of the 78 stories on the BBC website between 2012 and 2015 that mentioned 'Amazon' and 'tax avoidance', corporation tax paid by companies was misleadingly compared with sales revenues. Corporation tax is paid on profits and not on sales – which have nothing to do with the tax base for corporation tax. Indeed, it is worth noting that the tax as a proportion of turnover that the BBC pays on its commercial revenues is not very different from that of the companies that the BBC was criticising. Again, the *Guardian* reported this issue in a much more balanced way.

As noted above, bias exists in all organisations. Commercial news providers and those providing news funded by charitable trusts or other private forms of funding also exhibit biases. The question that needs to be addressed from a public policy point of view is why the position of the BBC is problematic.

The first problem is that the BBC has a huge share of the news and comment market, the size of which would lead to serious competition concerns if the BBC were a private organisation. Approximately 75 per cent of television news watched in the United Kingdom is provided by the BBC, for example.

Furthermore, those who fund the BBC have no choice in the matter. And the BBC is trusted, so its bias is more influential. Finally, the BBC has an interest in the political process and uses licence-payer funds to promote its view on the matter of how broadcasting should be funded.

While privatisation of the BBC would not guarantee the elimination of biases, it could lead the viewing public to be more appropriately sceptical. Privatisation (or, at least, a voluntary funding model) would also give the right of exit to those who do not wish to listen to the programmes broadcast by the BBC. Moreover, a privatised BBC would bear a considerable commercial cost if its reputation were impaired; thus, there would be an incentive to maintain it. This is especially true given the worldwide reach of the BBC.

The view is taken by many that reform of the BBC is the key to removing bias – perhaps through better oversight or regulation, for example. This overestimates the ability of politicians to design organisations from the outside to achieve the objectives they regard as desirable. Moreover, the following chapter by Stephen Davies suggests that reform is simply not possible. Institutional biases – which, in the case of the BBC, are not simple left versus right or socialist versus liberal biases – are deeply engrained within structures (such problems are not unique to the BBC, of course). Davies' chapter comes to the conclusion that competition and voluntary funding are the two essential reforms.

It is not bias as such that is the overriding problem. The main concerns should be with the institution's market power (especially in news provision), its non-voluntary funding method and its closeness to the political process. This combination is seriously problematic. The reforms proposed later in this book would not remove bias, but they would create a process of competition between institutions that were funded and owned in different ways, and which, therefore, had tendencies towards developing different forms of bias. The commercial and non-commercial production of broadcasting services could sit side-by-side, as long as they were funded on a voluntary basis. This happens in the newspaper industry (for example, many important blogs do not make money, and the *Guardian* and *Observer* are owned by a charitable trust). Furthermore, voluntary funding provides a discipline and also ensures that those who do not wish to be associated with or consume broadcasting services coloured by a particular set of views do not have to pay for them.

Privatising the BBC

This still leaves the question of what to do with the BBC. Tim Congdon deals with this in detail. Firstly, he reminds us that, though the BBC has huge market power in news provision, it is fast becoming a minnow in the international broadcasting, communication and entertainment world taken as a whole. Congdon believes that the BBC could, if it remains nationalised, become irrelevant. It needs to be liberated so that it can take advantage of recent and future technological developments.

It is impossible to imagine how developments will change broadcasting. Will the television become defunct? Will the laptop be replaced by the television? Will both be replaced by portable tablets or something we cannot today envisage? How vertically integrated should production, communication and broadcasting be? To what extent should there be horizontal integration between, for example, telecommunications companies and broadcasters? Keeping a publicly funded broadcaster, with a Charter drafted by politicians, risks seeing the BBC eclipsed by new technology in the same way that the Royal Mail has been eclipsed by email. There may well be a crucial role for the BBC in the future, but it needs to be free to discover it and free to raise the capital and current revenue to bring it to realisation. Already, the income from subscription to television broadcasters is twice the income from the licence fee received by the BBC.

Tim Congdon suggests the straightforward privatisation of the BBC on commercial terms. It would then be free to respond to the challenges of the future by developing whatever commercial relationships it wished with other organisations.

Indeed, the opportunities for an independent BBC are huge. The BBC has a trusted brand and an audience outside the UK that may already be ten times the size of its audience within the UK. The serving of an international audience financed by a domestic licence fee cannot be justified. For this reason, the BBC also seeks commercial income for its overseas services. But its commercial revenues are tiny compared with, for example, the revenues of Time Warner. And the overseas market will grow in importance relative to the domestic market as English becomes even more widely adopted as a second language internationally, and as demographic changes lead to population growth in key markets. In other words, there is an opportunity for the BBC to become a trusted, respected worldwide media organisation that is liberated to compete across a range of platforms and new technologies.

There are alternatives to Congdon's proposals. There could be privatisation without overt commercialisation. For example, the BBC could become a members' organisation like the National Trust, with the members being licence fee payers; of course, it could still have a commercial overseas arm. Or it could be set up with a large trust fund and operate with a governance structure, rather like the *Guardian*.

However, such organisations have well-known problems with regard to both corporate governance and raising capital. Mutually owned (customer-owned) organisations have historically had certain advantages in the financial services industry because they can resolve conflicts of interest between (say) customers and businesses. In retailing, cooperatives have helped to reduce the market power of suppliers. However, despite the fact that such organisations are often revered on the left (and those who believe in a free economy could have no objection to them in principle), recent examples, such as the Co-operative Bank and The Equitable Life Assurance Society, do illustrate their problems. With their corporate governance difficulties, mutuals or similar structures are hardly likely to be fleet of foot and able to respond to innovation. Non-shareholder models of ownership especially struggle when it comes to capital raising (again, this would be a huge constraint on the BBC in a rapidly changing world of media). The *Guardian* seems to have been able to keep up with technological change in the world of 'print' media (indeed, it has proven itself to be highly innovative and engaged with its customer base). However, its capital needs have, to a large degree, as Tim Congdon notes, been served by the sale of successful commercial ventures that it once owned.

At one time, the BBC was compared very favourably with overseas distributors and producers of television programmes, and it was argued that commercial disciplines had to be absent to ensure that there was not a 'dumbing down' of programming. Such an argument, once used against privatisation, is no longer tenable. Programmes such as *House of Cards*, *The Sopranos*, *The Wire* and *The Man in the High Castle* are, today, some of the most acclaimed television programmes or series, and they arise from models that have nothing close to that on which the BBC is based. Of course, anybody who has traced the development of culture in Britain would not be surprised to see that. Commercially viable plays, such as those by Shakespeare, as well as the public classical concert were innovations of the sixteenth and eighteenth centuries, respectively, which showed that culture can be commercially viable, popular and free of state influence and subsidy.

So, if the BBC is privatised, what happens to Channel 4? In many respects, it is a bit of a puzzle why Channel 4 remains owned by the government. Cento Veljanovski sees a possible role for a non-privatised BBC, but he believes that Channel 4 should be privatised. It would seem difficult to justify privatising the BBC while leaving Channel 4 as a nationalised business. There has been controversy about this recently, and a case can be made for ensuring that Channel 4 is independent of the state while exploring alternative arrangements for providing its capital and corporate governance. For example, perhaps it could be owned by its subscribers or by a trust (with additional capital being provided from the sale proceeds of the BBC).

The key issue is that broadcasting should be liberated from the state, and that the BBC is should not be constrained from maximising its impact and value as a result of its funding and ownership being tied to the state.

Conclusion

It is very difficult to justify the continued existence of the television licence, either in theory or in practice. It is an anachronism.

Furthermore, broadcasting is no longer a public good (if it ever was) – it is a club good that can be financed by subscription. If the licence fee does not survive, the next question is whether – and, if so, how – the state should finance PSB. The justifications for PSB (and, by implication, a state role in subsidising broadcasting) are becoming more and more tenuous. It is true that there may be externalities from the broadcasting of certain types of programmes, but these cannot be objectively evaluated, and they are not obviously greater than those from other forms of economic or cultural activity. The key to future policy in this area is surely to stop treating broadcasting as a separate activity. If a university, or a government entity such as the Arts Council, wishes to promote their mission through subsidising broadcasts or entering partnerships with broadcasters, they can do that. In other words, broadcasting – which itself is becoming ever-more difficult to define – is just one medium by which other objectives can be delivered, if they are desired and thought worthy of public subsidy.

The state ownership and subsidisation of broadcasting is especially problematic given the subjectivity of much broadcasting content. News, current affairs and a whole range of other content can be biased. This is not a problem unique to the BBC: all organisations have inherent biases within them. However, it can reasonably be argued that people should be free not to subscribe to services that have biases of which they do not approve; this points in the direction of a voluntary funding model. Furthermore, it can also be argued that the state should not be involved on such a large scale in something as sensitive as broadcasting. This points in the direction of privatisation of the BBC.

The huge potential reach of the BBC, together with its trusted brand and the importance of its being able to respond to the technological revolution all point in the direction of privatisation. Non-commercial or non-shareholder-owned models of privatisation might be possible, but they have serious limitations.

Alternative models could be tried with the smaller broadcaster Channel 4.

This proposal would liberate the BBC from the constraints that prevent it reaching its potential. The BBC is no longer a national organisation, and its focus is likely to become more international over time. It needs a business and ownership model more appropriate than the one designed the best part of 100 years ago.

References

Briggs, A. (1985) *The BBC – The First Fifty Years*. Oxford University Press.

CEA (2014) Change is in the air: US households viewing TV programming only via the Internet are poised to surpass those viewing only via antenna, finds new CEA study. https://www.ce.org/News/News-Releases/Press-Releases/2014/OTA-Study_060514.aspx

CEA (2015) Streaming devices poised to dominate viewing preferences as seven in ten viewers stream programming. https://www.ce.org/News/News-Releases/Press-Releases/2014/Streaming-Devices-Poised-to-Dominate-Viewing-Prefe.aspx

Gentleman, A. (2014) A day in court for non-payment of the TV licence. www.theguardian.com/society/2014/sep/24/in-court-non-payment-tv-licence-television-desperate-cases

Hearn, A. (2015) Netflix leads to record drops in US TV viewing. www.theguardian.com/technology/2015/feb/04/netflix-streaming-video-record-drops-in-us-tv-viewing

Parliamentary Papers (2015) www.publications.parliament.uk/pa/cm201415/cmselect/cmcumeds/315/31509.htm

Pirie, M. (2015) Non-payment of BBC licence fee accounts for 10% of all prosecutions. http://www.adamsmith.org/blog/blog/media-culture/non-payment-of-bbc-licence-fee-accounts-for-10-of-prosecutions

Plunkett, J. (2014) Offcom report identifies emerging 'generation gap' in young peoples' TV viewing. *Guardian*, 15 December. www.theguardian.com/media/2014/dec/15/facebok-tv-radio-ofcom-media

Rainey, S. (2015) How binge watching has changed TV for ever. www
.telegraph.co.uk/culture/tvandradio/11361212/How-binge-watch
ing-has-changed-TV-forever.html

Roettgers, J. (2015) Cable TV viewing declined by more than 12 percent
in January. https://gigaom.com/2015/02/03/cable-tv-viewing-declin
ed-by-more-than-12-percent-in-january/

Wolk, A. (2015) When Netflix and other on-demand services killed the
TV ad golden goose. www.theguardian.com/media-network/2015/
feb/05/netflix-subscription-services-television-ad-revenues

XStream (2015) Massive changes in TV viewing habits. http://xstream
.net/content/massive-changes-tv-viewing-habits

2 PUBLIC SERVICE BROADCASTING: OWNERSHIP, FUNDING AND PROVISION

Cento Veljanovski

No one has the right, and few the ability, to lure people into reading yet another analysis of PSB without a strong reason. The debate over PSB has raged for decades, and all that can be said, has been said, but it is not always clearly understood. The justification for this chapter is to reiterate an approach that has been accepted as the only coherent approach to broadcasting policy – consumer sovereignty. The Peacock Report, published in 1986, endorsed one of the core principles of economics – 'consumer sovereignty' – as the overriding objective of broadcasting policy (Peacock Report 1986: paragraph 592):

> British broadcasting should move towards a sophisticated market system based on consumer sovereignty. That is a system which recognises that viewers and listeners are the best ultimate judges of their own interests, which they can best satisfy if they have the option of purchasing the broadcasting services they require from as many alternative sources of supply as possible.

At the time of writing, the UK government is engaged in one of its periodic reviews of the BBC's Royal Charter and the licence fee. At such a time, the debate becomes polarised, fractious and more than usually other-worldly and emotional. Nonetheless, the PSB concept has retained its political support from successive governments, and recent commentators and even the government's Green Paper (DCMS 2015: 14) on the renewal of the BBC's Royal Charter perpetuate myths about the rationale and reality of PSB. As a result, the UK's terrestrial TV broadcast system continues to promote PSB. This is despite the economic case for PSB being weak, and weakening, due in particular to technological change. Nonetheless, the UK Government, even before its consultations have begun (DCMS 2015: 14), has concluded that: 'Despite technological change, there is still a strong rationale for the BBC continuing to exist in the twenty-first century.' What this 'strong rationale' is is not identified.

The other purpose of this chapter is to draw attention to the unique position of the IEA in fostering the economic analysis of broadcasting. In the UK and Europe, economists ignored the subject until the late 1990s. The notable, and eventually influential, exception has been IEA authors. The IEA was the first to publish papers on the economics of broadcasting and specifically to espouse the market approach to radio and TV broadcasting (Altman et al. 1962; Roberts 1965; Caine 1968) and cable TV (Veljanovski and Bishop 1983). IEA authors and supporters – notably, the late Sir Alan Peacock and Samuel Brittan, with, among others, the author of this chapter, an adviser to the Peacock Committee – have played a prominent part in fostering an economic approach, initially through the Peacock Committee report (1986) and in subsequent writings for the IEA, and in academic and popular publications (Veljanovski 1987a,b, 1990a,b, 2000).

Background

The concept of PSB is premised on a view that there is endemic market failure in the television or electronic video sectors. Left to itself, it is argued, the market would fail to provide the right balance of quantity, quality and scheduling of programming.

Further, it is suggested that the available programmes are skewed to those that are most commercially attractive.

In the UK, the justification for PSB evolved from one of administrative convenience to a market failure *qua* paternalistic view of the role of radio and then television in society. With the invention of the radio, the then Government nationalised the British Broadcasting Company in the late 1920s in order to create a vertically integrated monopoly, offering national radio broadcasts and then, with the availability of television sets, first one TV channel (BBC1) in 1937, and then a second national channel (BBC2) in 1965. During the latter half of the twentieth century, grudging concessions were made to commercial broadcasting. A heavily regulated commercial radio sector and one commercial advertiser-supported TV channel (ITV) was permitted in 1955, though this had heavy PSB and regional obligations. A publicly owned fourth channel (Channel 4 or C4) was later created in 1982 to complement the programming of ITV and to create an independent programme production sector. A fifth commercial broadcasting channel (Channel 5) was allowed as more spectrum was released (1997).

This structure of broadcasting, and even the term broadcasting, has been under threat for several decades now from two forces – liberalisation and technological change. For most of the last century, government regulation restricted radio and TV first to a monopoly, and then to a period of rationed or managed competition, as described above. Commercial radio was partially liberalised after the hard-fought battles during the Radio Caroline era in the 1960s showed that it could deliver what listeners wanted. The launch of ITV in the mid-1950s saw the BBC's audience share fall from 100 per cent to 30 per cent, sending shockwaves throughout the BBC and revealing that it had lost touch with its viewers. This caused a rapid change in its programme schedule towards more popular entertainment.

The second and more profound change has been technology and its commercial implications. In the 1980s and 1990s, the pressure to allow cable and satellite delivery systems and content to grow intensified. The first breach came in the 1980s, when Sky TV with the cooperation of a newly privatised British Telecom enabled Direct to Home (DTH) satellite pay TV signals to dish antennas using telecom satellites (Astra), rather than dedicated low capacity direct-broadcast satellites (the latter failing because of their low channel capacity and mismanagement). The advent of pay TV, the growth of cable and, more recently, the Internet and online video streaming services to computers, laptops, iPads and smartphones, coupled with developments in digital technology (optic fibre, compression and conditional access systems), means that lack of channel capacity is no longer a barrier to entry. These technologies are also challenging the whole idea of 'television' broadcasting as we know it, as well as the concept of a 'channel', as the proliferation of outlets, viewing patterns and formats alter dramatically.

The structure of public service broadcasting

Many think that the BBC represents the whole PSB sector. That is not the case (see Table 1). The terrestrial broadcasting system is peppered with PSB constraints and objectives. According to a UK Government website:[1]

> The UK has 5 public service television broadcasters. These broadcasters receive benefits like the licence fee (in the case of the BBC), guaranteed access to the spectrum (or section of the airwaves) they need for broadcasting, and prominence on

---

1   https://www.gov.uk/government/policies/making-it-easier-for-the-media-and
     -creative-industries-to-grow-while-protecting-the-interests-of-citizens/sup
     porting-pages/public-service-broadcasting

Table 1   **PSB channels and channels operated by public service broadcasters**

	Commercial PSBs' portfolio channels				
Main five PSB channels	BBC portfolio channels	ITV portfolio channels	Channel 4 portfolio channels	Channel 5 portfolio channels	Multichannels
BBC One	BBC Three	ITV+1	Channel 4+1	Channel 5+1	All other remaining channels
BBC Two	BBC Four	ITV2	E4	5*	
ITV	BBC HD	ITV2+1	E4+1	5*+1	
Channel 4*	BBC News	ITV3	More4	5 USA	
Channel 5	BBC Parliament	ITV3+1	More4+1	5 USA+1	
	CBeebies	ITV4	Film4	Channel 5+24	
	CBBC	ITV4+1	Film4+1		
	BBC Olympics channels	CITV	4Music		
	BBC red button channels	ITV Encore	4seven		
		ITV Encore+1	Channel 4 Olympics channels		
		ITVBe			
		ITVBe+1			

Channels include HD variants where applicable.
*Channel 4 data for 2009 includes S4C viewing. Following DSO Wales in 2010, Channel 4 data from 2010 relates to viewing to Channel 4 only.
Source: Ofcom (2015a, TV Viewing Annex).

TV electronic programme guides. In return they commit to providing services that give a benefit to the public, like news, local programming or cultural content.

The public service television broadcasters are:

- the BBC, a public corporation, funded mainly by the television licence fee;

- Channel 4, a public corporation self-funded by advertising;
- S4C, a public corporation, broadcasting in Wales and funded by a combination of BBC funding, government grant and advertising;
- Channels 3 and 5, whose licences are held by commercial television companies funded by advertising (currently for Channel 3, ITV in England and Wales, STV in Scotland and UTV in Northern Ireland).

These PSB organisations have expanded into the development of so-called (by the regulator Ofcom (Office of Communication)) PSB portfolio channels, often created to meet the commercial competition and take advantage of technological developments. This has led to concerns over the BBC's and C4's 'scale and scope' of operation: that is, whether they are trying to do too much, especially of a more commercial nature, in order to protect their market shares and political support.

Figure 1 shows the audience share (in viewing time) of the PSB channels and other broadcasters, including pay TV operators from 1988 to 2014.

The main channels of public service broadcasters have lost viewers' share from 100 per cent in 1991 to just over 51 per cent in 2014. The BBC has nonetheless retained a significant market share. BBC1 has declined from around 36 per cent in 1991 to 22 per cent in 2014. ITV has declined from 43 per cent in 1991 (then well above BBC1) to about 15 per cent in 2014. If BBC2 is added in, BBC1 and BBC2 had a collective viewer share of around 28 per cent in 2014 compared with 15 per cent for ITV/C3, around 5 per cent for C4 and 4 per cent for C5. In other words, the BBC has a viewing share significantly greater than the advertiser-supported 'PSB' competitors' core channels.

When the PSB portfolio channels are taken into account, the PSB channels have nearly a 72 per cent viewer share (Figure 2). The total BBC viewer share is 33 per cent, and the commercial

Figure 1   Viewer shares by channel (aged 4+), 1988–2014

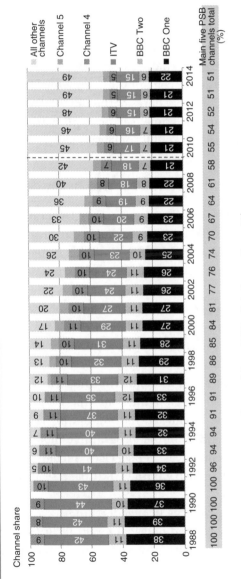

All values are given as percentages. Source: Ofcom (2015c, Data Annex, Figure 21).

PSB channels (ITV, C4 and C5), together with their respective portfolio channels, had a 39 per cent viewer share. But, if the viewing share is carved up between commercial PSBs (ITV and C5) and state-owned PSB channels (BBC and C4), then, remarkably, the state-owned channels have a viewer share of 44 per cent compared with 28 per cent for the commercial PSB channels. The continued high viewer shares of the BBC, PSBs and state-owned channels in a multichannel sector require an explanation, and raise competition and public policy issues.

What was and is public service broadcasting?

According to the BBC's first Director General, John Reith, the functions of the BBC were to 'educate, inform and entertain'. This trilogy remains part of the BBC's 'mission statement' today. Reith (1949) wrote that the responsibility of the BBC was to

> carry into the greatest number of homes everything that was best in every department of human knowledge, endeavour and achievement; and to avoid whatever was or might be hurtful.

While this contained a populist element, it was dominated by Reith's paternalistic view that only the right type of programming should be broadcast. Indeed, it was he who single-handedly turned the BBC into a 'programme monopoly' that stifled all alternative broadcasting services, including the then growing cable relay industry in the UK (Coase 1950; Veljanovski and Bishop 1983).

Obviously, given the licence fee funding of the BBC and the changing cultural and political forces in Britain, the BBC had to react and adapt its programming to accommodate these changes.

If one picks up the story of PSB in the late 1980s at the time of the Peacock Report (1986), there was a vigorous defence of

Figure 2   PSB and portfolio share of TV viewing, all individuals, by channel: 2004–14

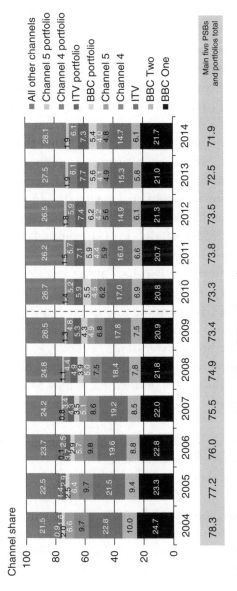

All values are given as percentages. Source: Ofcom (2015a, Figure 8).

PSB and the BBC against the possible incursion of more off-air channels, cable and satellite TV, and the threat to its licence fee funding. The BBC got off very lightly, as the attention of the Thatcher Government turned to ITV's bloated working practices, its monopoly of advertising and the large profits (monopoly rents) earnt by the then regional ITV franchise holders. It would be fair to say the Peacock Committee was misled on the possibility of a fifth channel (it was told one was not possible). It was also influenced by the evidence that the price elasticity of advertising was near unity, implying that there was a fixed advertising revenue 'pie' that would be fragmented if the BBC were forced to take advertisements (Veljanovski and Yarrow 1985). In the end, it decided to support some version of PSB with its preferred recommendation of an eventual arts council of the air (see further below).

The core tenets of PSB have never been pinned down in a convincing, operational way. The concept remains shrouded in vagueness, special pleading and *ex post* rationalisation, which mostly amounts to little more than the claim that PSB is what public service broadcasters do.

For example, in a Royal Television Society debate in Birmingham around the time of the Peacock Report, Michael Grade (then Chief Executive of Channel 4), said:

> My definition of PSB is producing a wide range of programmes which is free of any commercial consideration at the point of conception of the programme.

This was, of course, camouflage, since Channel 4 was broadcasting an increasing diet of commercial programmes (e.g. *Friends*), repeats and programmes designed to appeal to advertisers, so much so that it was effectively breaching its remit (Veljanovski 1994). The plain fact was and remains that the bulk of the programmes, and certainly those that attract most of the audiences of the five PSB channels, are programmes that could and do easily find a place in a commercially oriented television system.

In 1985, the Broadcasting Research Unit published *The Public Service Idea in British Broadcasting*, which enumerated eight principles of PSB:

1. geographic universality of reception from the four terrestrial channels;
2. catering for all interests and tastes;
3. catering for minorities;
4. concern for 'national identity and community';
5. detachment from vested interests and government;
6. one broadcasting system to be directly funded by the corpus of users;
7. competition in good programming rather than for numbers;
8. guidelines to liberate programme makers and not to restrict them.

These principles, even at the time, did not reflect the reality and trade-offs that had been made in support of PSB. For example, universal service – the requirement that everyone in the country receive the then all four channels – meant less local and regional programming, and less choice in the major urban areas.

One other principle was seen as paramount – that the BBC should be funded by the licence fee, so that it did not compete with the commercial broadcasters. The stated irrelevance of commercial considerations (at least in terms of funding) in the way the BBC programmed and scheduled its services was seen as the hallmark of PSB. Of course, today the BBC does not confine its funding to the licence fee, or its programmes to those which are purely PSB. Both conditions are violated, and the BBC has expanded and redesigned its services to meet the competition, and embraced commercial forces where convenient, such as in setting its own executives' salaries and in launching pay TV services. But, as will be argued below, the licence fee, while the 'best of the worst' forms of funding PSB, apart from pay-as-you-view, is a double-edged sword for the BBC that encourages it to compete with commercial broadcasters.

Notwithstanding this, in the three decades since the Peacock Report the definition of PSB has remained elusive. As Gavyn Davies (1999: 9) – an economist, who subsequently served as chairman of the BBC from 2001 to 2004 – stated in (yet) another report to the government:

> Some form of market failure must lie at the heart of any concept of public service broadcasting. Beyond simply using the catch-phrase that public service broadcasting must 'inform, educate and entertain', we must add 'inform, educate and entertain in a way which the private sector, left unregulated, would not do'. Otherwise, why not leave matters entirely to the private sector?

The Davies report (1999: 10) tellingly concluded: 'We decided that we may not be able to offer a tight new definition of PSB, but we nevertheless each felt that we knew it when we saw it'.

Ofcom (2004: 23), the UK communications regulator, noted:

> The problem with the term 'public service broadcasting' is that it has at least four different meanings: good television; worthy television; television that would not exist without some form of public intervention; and the institutions that broadcast this type of television.

Ofcom's (2005: paragraph 1.11) PSB review in 2005 set out what it could distil as the purposes and characteristics of PSB.

PSB purposes

- To inform ourselves and others and to increase our understanding of the world through news, information and analysis of current events and ideas.
- To stimulate our interest in and knowledge of arts, science, history and other topics through content that is accessible and can encourage informal learning.
- To reflect and strengthen our cultural identity through original programming at the UK, national and regional levels, on occasion bringing audiences together for shared experiences.
- To make us aware of different cultures and alternative viewpoints, through programmes that reflect the lives of other people and other communities, both within the UK and elsewhere.

PSB characteristics

- High quality – well funded and well produced.
- Original – new UK content, rather than repeats or acquisitions.
- Innovative – breaking new ideas or reinventing exciting approaches, rather than copying old ones.
- Challenging – making viewers think.
- Engaging – remaining accessible and enjoyed by viewers.
- Widely available – if content is publicly funded, a large majority of citizens need to be given the chance to watch it.

These, however, are high ideals to which most programme makers would subscribe.

Some years later, the House of Lords' (2009: paragraph 11) Communications Committee again commented on the ill-defined nature of PSB:

Nevertheless the interpretation of public service broadcasting as content that the market does not sufficiently provide is gaining increasing support. It implies a focus on defining the core elements of public service provision that should, as a matter of public policy, continue to be supported. Such elements might include, for example, national and regional news, current affairs programmes, the arts, children's programming, programmes dealing with religion and other beliefs and UK content.

Where does the PSB concept stand today?

The BBC is self-governing through the BBC Trust and is accountable to Parliament. The BBC's Royal Charter (2007–15) defines its mission, purpose and values. It sets out six broad public purposes of the BBC:

1. sustaining citizenship and civil society;
2. promoting education and learning;
3. stimulating creativity and cultural excellence;
4. representing the UK, its nations, regions and communities;
5. bringing the UK to the world and the world to the UK;
6. delivering to the public the benefit of emerging communications technologies and services.

The *Communications Act 2003* (Section 265) sets out in general terms the PSB remits of the commercial PSB channels. Section 265(2) defines the PSB remit for Channels 3 and 5 as 'the provision of a range of high quality and diverse programming'. For Channel 4 (Section 265(3)), it is 'the provision of a broad range of high quality and diverse programming which, in particular:

(a) demonstrates innovation, experiment and creativity in the form and content of programmes;

(b) appeals to the tastes and interests of a culturally diverse society;

(c) makes a significant contribution to meeting the need for the licensed public service channels to include programmes of an educational nature and other programmes of educative value; and

(d) exhibits a distinctive character.'

All PSB channels are subject to varying degrees of oversight by the telecoms regulator, Ofcom. Under the Communications Act, it is charged with producing a periodic review of whether the public service broadcasters (the BBC, the Welsh Authority, C4, ITV and the public teletext provider), taken together, are fulfilling the purposes of PSB. In the case of C4 and ITV, Ofcom sets programme quotas as part of its licensing function.

The level of external regulation has increased, although in some cases (ITV) the PSB obligations have decreased. In 2010, parliament made substantial changes to the remit and governance arrangements of C4 through the Digital Economy Act 2010 (DEA). In particular, the DEA introduced a new remit for C4 in relation to its provision of media content, to be delivered via its portfolio channels, on-demand and Internet services as well as through Channel 4. The Act also introduced a separate reporting and governance process, under which C4 is now required to prepare an annual Statement of Media Content Policy (SMCP) on how its remit has been delivered in the last year, and will be delivered in the next year, across its services.

Overall, the definition of PSB has developed in a rather chameleon-like way to fit the political economy debates of the day. PSB is certainly alive and well as a public policy objective, as we can see from the regulatory structures now in place. The current justification for PSB normally relates back to some kind of market failure argument that is also used to justify other interventions. The concept of market failure in broadcasting therefore needs further analysis.

Market failure

The Davies Report (1999: Annex 8) on the future funding of the BBC listed a number of what it described as 'market failures', which could arguably underpin PSB, and which many saw and still see as endemic in the broadcasting sector, together with those which would arise in a digital age. These were the following:

Sources of market failure

- broadcasting is a public good;
- quality broadcasting is a merit good;
- consumers are not fully informed;
- broadcasting produces externalities;
- economies of scale exist in broadcasting;
- spectrum scarcity.

Will market failure persist with new broadcasting technology?

- over-concentration in the market/risk of private monopoly;
- economies of scale will increase;
- economies of scope will increase;
- gateways bottlenecks may exist;
- increased audience fragmentation;
- negative externalities may increase.

Existing market failures

The list of existing market failures is far from convincing. Let me deal with these in a different order, reflecting their historical importance in the evolution of PSB.

Firstly, spectrum scarcity. The original reason for a nationalised BBC monopoly had nothing to do with cultural values or inadequate programme quality and diversity. It was an administrative solution to the perceived threat of radio frequency interference or congestion – or, as it was colourfully put at the time, 'bedlam of the airwaves' (Coase 1947, 1948, 1950, 1954). There was a growing concern that the commercial use of spectrum would lead to radio interference and congestion, thus reducing the sound quality and reception of radio services. More importantly, it would challenge the Post Office's monopoly of wireless telegraphy. The bureaucratic solution proposed by the Post Office was to nationalise the then British Broadcasting Company, which had been set up by radio manufacturers as a way to increase sales of their wireless sets.[2] Commercial radio was prohibited. The idea was that, if there were a statutory monopoly service, then the technical interference problems could be dealt with by internal administrative means through government departments or other government bodies.

Of course, airwave scarcity and congestion were not market failures in themselves but the direct consequence of the refusal to establish property rights and a market in radio spectrum bandwidth. As Coase (1959, 1960) showed, and as is recognised and accepted today, the solution is to define property rights in bandwidth and allow these to be enforced as one does land, physical and intellectual property rights. While this may have been a

---

2   The original shareholders were British Thomson-Houston, General Electric, Marconi, and Metropolitan-Vickers.

bit more complicated and required some technological advances, it was not a market failure in itself.

The nationalisation of the airwaves had very adverse consequences in creating a programme monopoly, denying the entertainment and information services that many wanted. It also led to the squandering of the radio spectrum on inefficient uses, often by government departments, state monopoly entities and the civil and military defence forces – spectrum was allocated to the wrong people/entities for the wrong purposes. The auctioning of ITV/Channel 3 franchises in the late 1980s, and then 3G mobile licences in the 1990s, together with the increasing acceptance that spectrum could be sold and traded, has led to the release of more spectrum and its reassignment to more commercially valuable uses.

Notwithstanding this, today, despite the privileged position of the BBC and C4 in obtaining spectrum free of charge, these services are transmitted using a variety of platforms, including digital terrestrial, satellite, cable and the Internet (Figure 3).

Figure 3 How PSB channels are delivered to viewers, 2014

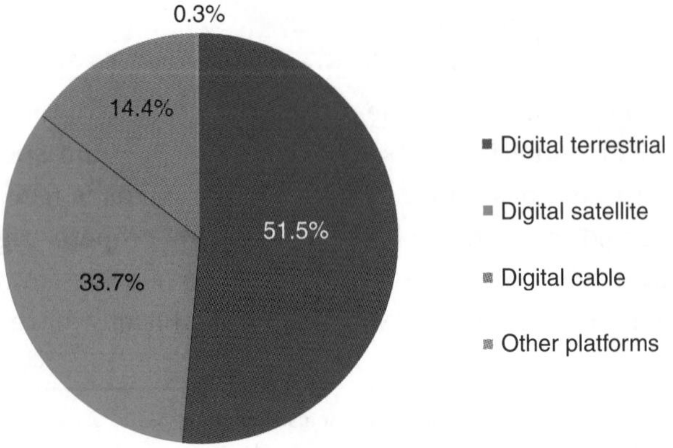

Source: Ofcom (2015a, Figure 33).

These platforms or delivery systems do not suffer from limited channel capacity.

Another argument deployed by Davies is that broadcasting is a public good. This term has a specific technical meaning in economics. It is a good or service where the consumption by one individual does not subtract or reduce the consumption of others, and where exclusion is not feasible. A television programme that has a fixed cost of production, once produced, and broadcast can be seen by an additional viewer at zero cost, could be thought of as a public good. Thus, the 'efficient' price is zero: equal to the near negligible marginal costs of transmitting a television programme to an additional viewer. Under these cost and pricing constraints, a commercial operator would not produce programmes, and, if it charged, it would lead to the 'inefficient' under-consumption of programmes.

The use of the public goods argument in television and video services, especially today, is disingenuous. Indeed, it always misrepresented the argument, because marginal cost pricing is not efficient, as it fails to take into account fixed production and distribution costs. It does not take an economic genius to appreciate that, if the price were zero, nothing would be produced. The theory, not the pricing, is wrong. In addition, a public good should not be given away free, as is often implied, but each consumer should be charged a price that reflects his or her marginal valuation. That is, there should, if possible, be a market consisting of differential pricing. The obstacle to this is allegedly the inability to get people to pay because of the absence of an encryption and payment technology. However, this technology has always existed, but it was abandoned to protect the BBC as early as the 1920s. More to the point, such payment systems exist today and are in widespread use, allowing pay TV to flourish. In technical terms, what might at one time have been a public good is now a club good – exclusion is possible and payment can be enforced. Finally, video programmes are created and sold in markets; even the BBC sells its programmes in markets, and, after the Hollywood studios, it is the biggest distributor of television programmes in the world. Like spectrum scarcity, the public goods argument is simply an observation deployed selectively to justify a position already reached on other grounds, i.e. those of Reithian paternalism.

But, what is more to the point is that the market failure case disappears when a genuine market in programmes can be developed. Pay TV is that market. Add to this the fact that the whole concept of a channel is fast becoming redundant, as people dip in and out of different video media and have access to interactive online services, and one sees a fragmented but vibrant market in video and online services. This far outstrips that predicted by even the maddest visionary in the 1980s.

The Green Paper's (DCMS 2015: 14) only justification for the BBC is that 'high quality PSB content has generally been seen as a "merit good", which would be under-provided in a free market', continuing:

> PSBs such as the BBC still deliver positive effects for society such as extending democratic knowledge through news and current affairs, helping extend the UK's influence and reputation abroad, addressing needs of audiences such as minority language groups, and serving audiences (such as children) where excessive advertising would be inappropriate. These goods would not be provided in sufficient volume by the market alone.

The argument that broadcasting is a merit good is paper thin. A merit good in economics is a vague and ill-defined concept, which has been largely discredited. It has been defined as a good whose value exceeds the valuation an individual would place upon it. This is presumably related to the value that a 'fully informed' consumer would place on it. It is hard to see how this concept differs from the externality argument, and how it has universal appeal. The best argument is that potential viewers may under-value education and informative programming, and over-value entertainment. However, sport has been treated until recently as a crucial aspect of PSB, so much so that major international events were 'listed', meaning they had to be shown on the BBC or ITV (Veljanovski 2000). The merit good argument sheds no light on who this fully informed consumer, who makes judge-ments about the externalities or true value of a good programme, would be. Is it the political class or some kind of bureaucracy? Why are their views more valid than those who watch television? If the mass of consumers is incapable of judging whether a tele-vision programme is of sufficient value, are they in a position to judge who should be the politicians that are making policy about broadcasting? Might those who are making judgements about merit goods not have their own prejudices (see the chapters on bias) that are not related to some kind of objective criteria about the value of a programme?

The merit goods argument suffers from another drawback. To many people, television is a 'de-merit good' that has led to the de-cline of reading, conversation, manners, eating habits, family life and so on. While the economists' theory can extol the drawbacks of the market in supplying more TV, others would and do regard any supposed failure on this score as a good thing.

The existence of economies of scale in broadcasting is again not unique to broadcasting. If the suggestion is that broadcast-ing is, as a result, a natural monopoly or duopoly, then it is wrong, and symptomatic of the tendency to view the PSB organisations in isolation from developments elsewhere in the communica-tions sector.

The other causes of market failure are simply variations of those already discussed. Even if they were correct, their quanti-tative significance has not been measured; nor do they justify the structure of PSB that has evolved, which inhibited competition and technological developments in broadcasting for decades.

Another source of market failure not mentioned is the claim that direct competition between media outlets may lead to duplication of common denominator programming. This was based on the theory, which has a good economic pedigree, that a few free-to-air (i.e. advertiser-supported) competitive channels would maximise their audience share by broadcasting the same type of programming. Like the ice cream sellers along the beach promenade described by Hotelling (1920), broadcasters would find that they could maximise their audience share by locating next to one another and producing the same mediocre programming. But the theory applied at best to advertiser-supported television (Steiner 1952; Beebe 1977; Spence and Owen 1997), and it was not applicable to a genuine market in programming with a large number of providers or to pay TV. Furthermore, this theory evaluated television and broadcasting against the consumer sovereignty objective, something PSB advocates rejected. It also ignored the very simple fact that advertiser-supported TV had an important role to play, both as entertainment and to advertise industries' wares, and generated massive consumers' surplus for viewers who received the programmes free of charge.

It is not necessary to go into the assumptions and qualifications of the programming 'inefficiencies' of duopoly channel advertiser-supported broadcasting markets. Suffice it to say that, as the number of channels increases, and if the audience is diverse, even commercial advertiser-supported channels will not slavishly broadcast the same lowest-common-denominator programming. But, more to the point, the *bête noir* of supporters of PSB – American network television – was portrayed as a cultural wasteland, which careful research showed was not the case (Gallagher 1989). This is evident from the popularity and production standards of American network television programmes and the fact that they are now shown on British PSB and commercial channels.

The paradox of PSB (see Veljanovski 1988b, 1989e) is that its past and present structure does not maximise programme diversity. It is a hybrid structure that harnesses commercial programming in order to effectively cross-subsidise the provision of what is deemed PSB. In the case of the BBC, this is done by broadcasting a large quantity of popular programmes bought from the US as well as other programming on BBC1 in order to maintain its viewer share and thereby justify the universal licence fee. This programming could easily be profitably shown on commercial television stations without any PSB remit. Moreover, it is obvious that if the BBC devoted most of its funds to programme production and scheduling different to that shown on commercial free-to-air services, much more diversity could be introduced into the terrestrial broadcast segment for the same licence fee revenues. As will be described later, such a reform is relatively easily done without too much structural change to the present terrestrial PSB system.

Taken as a whole, the market failures case for PSB is weak. One may not like what the market produces and regard the Internet as crass and demeaning, but these opinions are largely a commentary on peoples' tastes and often reflect an elitist attitude. This is not to say that the pay TV and related markets work perfectly or would necessarily replicate the programming that would be generated and broadcast by PSB. But it is not the role of the market to replicate what is arbitrarily defined by the BBC or others commissioning PSB programmes, nor is it the function of the BBC and C4 to largely duplicate programming that would otherwise find a place on unregulated commercial video-delivery systems (Veljanovski 1999a,b, 2001).

Furthermore, what is often missing from the debate, and even more serious analysis, is a recognition of the inefficiencies associated with the broadcast rationing and regulation that underpin the UK's PSB system. The Thatcher Government and the Peacock Committee were shocked by the inefficiency of ITV, and, more recently, the profligacy of the BBC has come to light.

Future market failures

There is also rather a weak case for the 'future market failures' that were laid out by Davies. That the new digital age will fragment audiences there is no doubt, but that is hardly a market failure. That it will lead to the emergence of new bottlenecks and gateways, and that the cost conditions of transmission and content may allow some owners of delivery networks to gain first-mover advantages and large market shares is also true. But these are concerns now dealt with by competition law and industry regulation. They are no different from those confronting the mining or mobile telephony sectors.

This is not to say that some of the issues raised by the new media are not difficult; for a time, they will seem intractable as new technologies and business models move from infancy to maturity. At first, pay TV, the Internet, mobile Internet and so on were seen as the precursors of competition, and then as threats to competition, thus attracting regulation and controls as the dynamics of the market were recognised. The relevant issues generally relate to gateways and access to key delivery systems or technologies as well as, in the formative years, the somewhat destructive winner-takes-all competition between operators (such as that which existed between Sky and BSB in the 1990s) to gain dominance of the sector. But, these are part of the process of competition that is common when there is radical technical change in any commercial sector. It is a necessary driver of innovation and a process of discovery of consumers' needs.

The reality of the development of new media has been a struggle against entrenched interests and the retardation of competing technologies and commercial services. For example, one of the pressure groups lobbying for control of radio in the 1920s was the newspapers, who wanted to limit a threat to their news services. As commercial broadcasting and the new media developed, existing media owners fought hard to block entry and took steps to control the media, leading to predictable concerns about cross-media ownership and 'share of voice'. These concerns have often been over-egged and are due largely to the way PSB and broadcasting regulation fostered monopoly and then oligopolistic media market structures that gave one organisation a larger 'voice' not justified on competitive and diversity grounds.

The transformation of the communications sector due to technological innovation has gathered pace in the last decade. There has been a move from analogue to digital transmission, and the development of compression technology, which has increased channel capacity, has brought down costs, reduced barriers to entry and so on. Furthermore, the development and widespread availability of encryption technology and conditional access systems enables channels and programmes to be scrambled so that payment can be required, thus leading to the growth of pay TV. While cable systems were banned to support BBC TV prior to the 1980s, they now proliferate with ample channel capacity. Online services such as YouTube, Netflix and general video streaming, taken together with the changing viewing patterns and practices of the younger generation, have meant that the role of video entertainment and information is altering dramatically. It is no longer a matter of catering for a given demand but of developing and responding to new delivery technologies and different ways of offering video entertainment. As a result, the type and range of content available from commercial providers has proliferated.

So, with regard to the possible future justifications for PSB made by Davies, these are really not justifications for PSB at all. Rather, they are largely an observation that changing technology may give rise to competition concerns, as happens in other industries when there is rapid innovation. There are already mechanisms to deal with these problems, and promoting the market power of the incumbents in the face of competition from innovation is not an appropriate way forward.

Can a case be for public service broadcasting?

The analysis above may seem overstated. It might be argued that there is a range of programmes that may not survive in a competitive, fully commercialised communications sector. However, this does not indicate market failure, and it is far from clear what such programmes might be. The House of Lords' Communications Committee quoted above suggested that programmes under-provided by the market might be 'national and regional news, current affairs programmes, the arts, children's programming, programmes dealing with religion and other beliefs and UK content'. Most of these are produced and shown in large quantities by the market, and do not seem to me distinctively uncommercial.

Recent research for Ofcom (Enders Analysis 2014) shows that the fast-developing online media offers 'hundreds if not thousands of online media services that provide content which could be regarded as PSB content compared to the five PSBs. This content ranged from sport and leisure, actual current affairs, news. The gaps were in cultural affairs and religion' (Figure 4).

Notwithstanding this, if there is a case for PSB, it needs to be clearly identified, and the reasons why the relevant programmes would not be produced and transmitted by the market need to be fully justified. If such programming exists, then it is important that it is funded and transmitted in ways that do not distort the whole broadcasting system or require funding that is disproportionate. The cosy duopoly of the BBC and ITV/C3 prior to the 1990s resulted in significant inefficiencies. Moreover, the present structure of PSB crowds out programming that would otherwise be produced by the commercial sector, and represents unfair competition with the commercial sector. Competition issues are discussed further in Box 1.

Figure 4 **Public service broadcasting by non-public-service broadcasters**

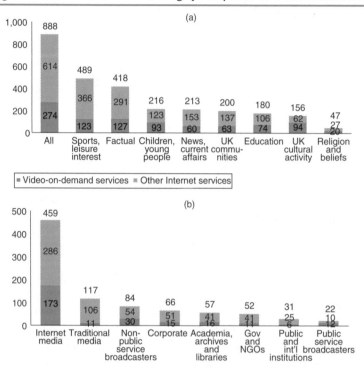

(a) Online media services by public service objective, June 2014. (b) Online media services by organisation type, June 2014. Source: Enders Analysis (2014).

Funding of PSB

Suppose for a moment that a case can be made out for some form of PSB. How should it be funded?

The current funding of PSB takes or has taken a variety of forms – the licence fee, cross-subsidisation from advertising within a channel (ITV) and across channels (ITV to C4) and direct subsidy (BBC World Service, until recently, and Gaelic language programmes in Scotland). In addition, the BBC, C4 and

Box 1   Competition policy and the BBC

The BBC and other PSBs are subject to general and specific competition laws. They must comply with both EU and UK law and competition interventions administered by Ofcom as well as, in the case of the BBC, self-imposed fair trading rules.

State aid and the licence fee

The area of competition law most relevant to the licence fee debate is state aid. Over the last several decades, the competition regulators have received many complaints and undertaken investigations alleging that the funding of PSBs across Europe constitutes illegal state aid. Despite the general prohibition against state aid, in some circumstances government interventions that are necessary for a well-functioning and equitable economy can be exempt. Therefore, the European Treaty leaves room for a number of policy objectives for which state aid can be considered compatible.

In the PSB sector, the Commission has tended to exempt the BBC from state aid rules. For example, in May 2002 the European Commission investigated whether the funding of the BBC's digital television and radio stations was illegal state aid. The Commission concluded that it was not, as it gave the BBC 'no real advantage' because the 'compensation for the digital channels is not disproportionate to the net costs of the new channels, which are performed as part of the public service obligations of the BBC' (European Commission 2002). Similarly, in 1999 BSkyB complained to the European Commission that the public funding for the BBC's 24-hour television news channel was illegal state aid. This was rejected by the European Commission on the ground that EU rules allowed such aid if it was compensation for the delivery of services of general economic interest, as entrusted to member states. The Commission found that the financial means granted to the channel did not exceed its actual costs, and so were proportionate to the public service.

A contrary view

However, this formulation of the state aid rules presupposes acceptance of the objectives of PSB and the BBC's expansion (in the case cited above), which may themselves distort competition. The premise of this chapter is that the activities of PSBs is overextended and inherently distortionary. For example, BBC Radio One is the most-listened-to radio station, and BBC News Online is the most-watched news website. These satisfy the state aid rules but at the same time clearly distort the market, as they compete with commercial broadcasters providing the same commercial content, thereby crowding-out commercial broadcasters from these areas because the competition is too intense.

Competition in production

Regulatory and competition interventions have also been prominent to foster more competition in production. At various times, the BBC (and other PSB providers) have been required to increase commissioning of programmes from external producers. For example, as part of the last licence fee settlement the BBC agreed to commission up to 50 per cent of its programmes from such external producers.

Competition in news provision

Two other areas where legitimate competition concerns could be raised are in relation to local news provision and the influence on the news agenda more generally. It has long been argued by local newspapers that the BBC's dominant position, financed by a compulsory licence fee, involves unfair competition with local news. The BBC contests this claim. More recently, the local newspaper industry has claimed that BBC proposals to create a shared service with local newspapers to cover local courts and councils will represent unfair competition. This issue is complex. If the move is seen as a competitive threat to local newspapers, it could indeed be regarded as anti-competitive. On the other hand, the 'shared service' will involve the BBC providing local newspapers with some of their content. Given that this is financed by the licence fee, local newspapers would be receiving a subsidy from the licence fee that could be regarded as state aid under EU law.

When it comes to media ownership, there are rules that severely limit the ownership of television channels and newspapers to prevent dominance of the news sector by one provider. However, there are no equivalent rules that deal with the dominance of the BBC in news provision. Despite the relative decline of the BBC in broadcasting in general, it is dominant in news provision. In a recent Ofcom survey, five of the top eight news providers were BBC sources, with BBC One way out in front as the number one source.[1] Such market power would not be allowed if the BBC were a private organisation or in the newspaper market.

Conclusion

This is not a full analysis of competition issues. What is apparent is that the competition rules, by accommodating PSB objectives, provide only limited controls on the BBC, and

---

1   See http://stakeholders.ofcom.org.uk/binaries/research/tv-research/
    news/2015/News_consumption_in_the_UK_2015_report.pdf

> leave intact the structural and behavioural abuses. These
> often require additional *ex ante* rules and regulation to con-
> trol. The BBC should operate under the same law as applies to
> other broadcasters and news providers.

S4C receive a subsidy, as they do not pay for spectrum. Thus, as a
practical matter, PSB can be and is funded in different ways.

The bulk of the funds for PSB comes from the licence fee paid
by each viewing household, which goes to the BBC. This is a hypothecated tax levied on the ownership of television sets and
other receiving devices used for live viewing of the BBC. It provided the BBC with revenue of £3.7 billion in 2014 (see Figure 5).
This is supplemented from other activities, but largely from the
sale of BBC programmes (£1 billion), giving the BBC Group a
total income of around £5 billion. Indeed, BBC Worldwide is the
largest TV programme distributor outside the large Hollywood
studios.

The BBC's funding has come under pressure over the last
decade. The licence fee increases have been capped to the rate
of inflation and have been eroded by the so-called iPlayer loop-
hole; more viewers receive the service using catch-up services,
which do not attract a licence fee. At the same time, the government has imposed increased responsibilities and costs on the
BBC. In the 2010 licence fee settlement between the government
and the BBC, the BBC agreed to fund the World Services (which
had hitherto been funded by the Foreign Office), BBC Monitoring, S4C, local television infrastructure and the roll-out of
super-fast broadband through Broadband Delivery UK. Following the 2015 Budget, the BBC will fund the free licence given to
over 75s. This squeeze on finances is symptomatic of concerns
over the scale and scope of the BBC, and whether the licence fee

income is being used simply to show what could otherwise be shown on commercial services. Notwithstanding this, the issue of the extent of funding of the BBC is a critical one, raised by the lack of support for a market failure case for the BBC outlined above.

While there is considerable opposition to the licence fee as a means of funding PSB, it has several attractions over funding from general taxation revenues, which is mooted in the Green Paper on the BBC Charter Review (DCMS 2015). This is because the licence fee creates a link between the viewer, the BBC and politicians. The viewer can indirectly exert constant pressure on the politicians and the BBC by complaining about the level of the licence fee and the programming output of the BBC. If the BBC were funded from general tax revenues, this link would be broken, and the pressures and constraints on the BBC and politicians would be severed.

However, the licence fee does have a number of unattractive and perverse features.

It has been described as a regressive compulsory poll tax. Its compulsory nature is widely disliked by viewers. Whether it is in fact regressive is a moot point, because its incidence has to be compared with the viewing patterns of those paying it, to see if it is disproportionately affecting low income groups who watch little BBC television and radio. The non-payment of the licence fee is a criminal offence. Indeed, almost 200,000 viewers a year have been prosecuted and liable to a fine up to £1,000 and a criminal record. There have been 50 people jailed. This represents an incredible 10 per cent of all criminal prosecutions in the UK. The present government has announced that it will decriminalise non-payment of the licence fee, but there are signs that its commitment to this proposal is wavering.

The periodic review of the licence fee is a ritualised and highly politicised affair, either extolling the virtues of the BBC or criticising the BBC's performance, political bias and poor internal governance. The compulsory nature of the licence fee means that the BBC is not subject to the same economic constraints as the commercial broadcasters, especially the procyclical volatility of advertising revenues that fund ITV and C4 (see Figure 5). The BBC does not have to compete for revenues, and, within each licence fee period, has a guaranteed income, which has been rising in nominal terms compared with the decline in advertising revenues of the commercial broadcasters (Figure 5). This places it in a financially and competitively stronger position than ITV during cyclical downturns. This contrasts with the position of pay TV operators, who have increased their audience share and revenues significantly.

But there is a fundamental paradox at the heart of the licence fee in that its strong feature is it weakest. It has been noted above that the licence fee has the attractive feature of linking viewers to the BBC and politicians. They are annually reminded that they are paying for a 'free' service and can protest if they do not regard it as value for money. But the licence fee 'forces' the BBC to offer a broad-based service that attracts a relatively high audience/viewing share, otherwise popular and political support for the fee would drain away. This, in turn, results in the BBC broadcasting vast quantities of programming that would have been shown by commercial broadcasters. It has to satisfy the viewers and listeners with a broad mix of programming delivered in different ways, otherwise it would be marginalised as a broadcasting institution. This tendency to have broad appeal and meet the competition dilutes its PSB role. It generates an expansionist strategy, which has increased the scope and scale of the BBC's activities and thereby blurs its contribution to PSB. While for the BBC's management this makes sense – competent, ambitious managers do not want to oversee decline and be restrained – it undermines the case for the BBC. The objective of policy in relation to PSB should not be to ensure the survival of the BBC as it is now or its growth as a viable competitor to the commercial broadcasters. The BBC and PSB are not synonymous – the policy goal for those who support

Figure 5 Total TV revenues by source, 2009–14

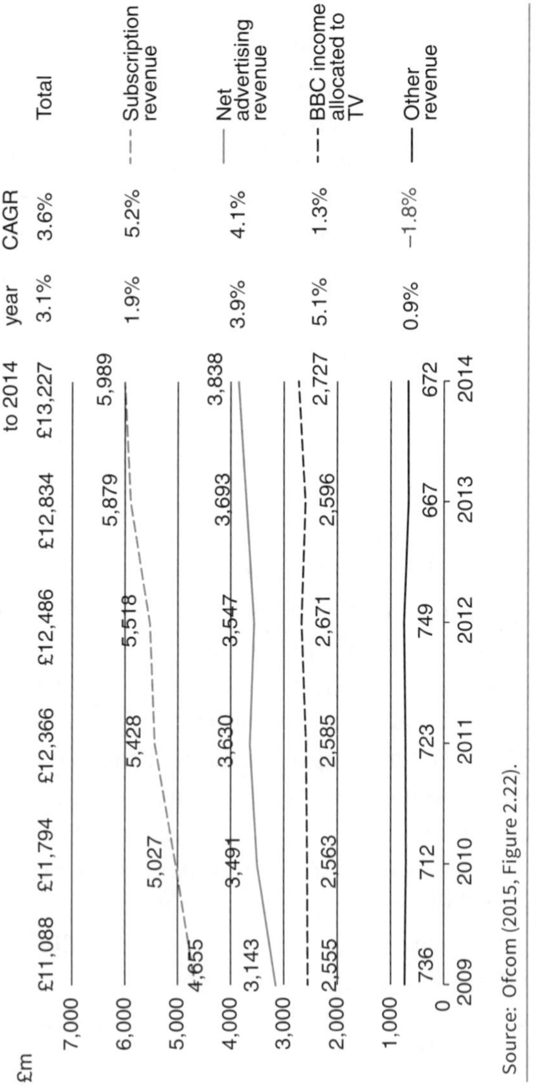

£m	2009	2010	2011	2012	2013	2014 / Growth to 2014	One year	Five-year CAGR	
Total	£11,088	£11,794	£12,366	£12,486	£12,834	£13,227	3.1%	3.6%	Total
Subscription revenue	4,655	5,027	5,428	5,518	5,879	5,989	1.9%	5.2%	Subscription revenue
Net advertising revenue	3,143	3,491	3,630	3,547	3,693	3,838	3.9%	4.1%	Net advertising revenue
BBC income allocated to TV	2,555	2,563	2,585	2,671	2,596	2,727	5.1%	1.3%	BBC income allocated to TV
Other revenue	736	712	723	749	667	672	0.9%	−1.8%	Other revenue

Source: Ofcom (2015, Figure 2.22).

PSB is the efficient provision of PSB content, and not the preservation of the BBC.

Yet the real criticism of the licence fee is that, in the current broadcasting environment, it is increasingly hard to justify. Technologies now enable the viewer to be charged for their programmes, and there is a variety of devices – over-the-air TV, cable, Internet and mobile devices – which can download and be used to view live video programming.

PSB can be and is funded by advertising, as C4 and other advertiser-supported channels have shown. However, to permit the BBC to take advertising would unleash a large state-owned competitor on ITV and C5. This would severely reduce their advertising revenues and damage their viability, even if the BBC did not alter its programming. Paradoxically, advertising markets are peculiar in that the supply side is more or less fixed by the advertising exposures to viewers that can be generated. Thus, the principle effect of increased channels and advertising is simply to fragment the audience while leaving the aggregate volume of exposures constant. Indeed, channels that can supply large viewer share can charge relatively more than several channels supplying the same volume of exposures. Research for the Peacock Committee (Yarrow and Veljanovski 1988) and more recent research confirms that the price elasticity of demand for advertising is near unity, implying that the television advertising pie is more or less fixed.

Structural reforms

Unreformed sectors are an anachronism

The other big question is how the provision of core PSB programmes should be organised. Should it be the preserve of two state-owned broadcasters (the BBC and C4/S4C) and several others with specific PSB obligations? Or should core PSB programming be dispersed over the broadcasting sector funded by an Arts Council–type organisation, with funds made available for whichever media companies bid in a competitive (more recently referred to as 'contestable funding') process? Or is the case for PSB so weak as to permit radical structural reform and privatisation of PSBs without any funding mechanism or other intervention being used to promote PSB?

Firstly, it should be noted that the state ownership of major broadcasters is an anachronism in a free society. As discussed above, the historical reasons for this structure were dubious even at the time they were advanced. But, as the PSB system developed, it created three state-owned entities (the BBC, C4 and S4C), which actively competed for viewers and also advertising revenue (in the case of C4) with commercial broadcasters. State ownership and the licence fee have generated major distortions together with internal governance problems at the BBC. There is a clear case in today's communications environment for slimming down and privatising segments of the PBS system.

There has already been significant structural reform in the sector. ITV and parts of the BBC have vertically disintegrated by closing down their programme production facilities, and they are required (by regulation) to buy in all or a large proportion of their programmes. The terrestrial transmission systems once owned by the communications regulator (the then IBA for ITV and C4) and the BBC have been privatised and are now operated by a separate entity. The ITV/C3 network, which was operated by a number of regional franchise companies, has now consolidated by takeovers. Based on the Peacock Report (1986) recommendations, the original regional ITV operators were selected by competitive cash bids in 1989–90, thus paying and establishing property rights in spectrum (although spectrum cannot, as it can in the US, be freely traded other than by a takeover of ITV).

Future reforms

The most obvious first step relates to C4. There is little justification for a state-owned C4. The origin of C4 came from the intense lobbying by independent programme producers to create an independent programme production sector and increase programme diversity. This rationale has now largely disappeared. The auction franchising process inspired by the Peacock Committee resulted in the then regional ITV franchise holders divesting themselves of programme making, diminishing the case for the C4 model.

The coexistence of the BBC, and in particular BBC1 and C4, is anachronistic. BBC1 is a mass audience channel, showing a vast quantity of commercial programmes funded by the licence fee under the umbrella of PSB. C4's programme remit is to offer diverse and innovative programming, catering for tastes not well served by the other main advertiser-supported broadcaster. In fact, programme diversity and innovation could be maximised by switching the remits of BBC1 and C4. The large bulk of PSB programming would then be broadcast by the BBC, and the BBC would withdraw from acquiring, funding and broadcasting popular commercial programming.

Such proposals, first made 25 years ago (Veljanovski 1988b, 1989: 109–11), were heavily criticised at the time as having the potential to turn the BBC into a 'cultural ghetto'. However, they could turn the BBC (using a similar emotive metaphor) into a 'cultural oasis' focused on programmes that would not be broadcast in sufficient quantity in the commercial sector. This would pave the way for the privatisation of C4 (Veljanovski 1996).

A more radical proposal would be to privatise the BBC. While this has an appeal in principle, the consequence would be to unleash a large former state broadcaster to compete for advertising and subscription revenues with the existing terrestrial and commercial media companies. Any such privatisation would have to be accompanied by slimming down the BBC, and this would pose commercial and organisational challenges. A slimmed down BBC would not be as commercially valuable, and, hence, the sale price would be reduced to the government. There would also be issues surrounding the ownership of the BBC programme library.[3]

An alternative proposal is the arts council for the air, as described by Peacock (2004). This requires a clear operational definition of PSB and its funding, but it would harness competitive forces in the production and delivery of PSB programming. This could operate in many ways. It could, for example, provide grants to allow broadcasters to adapt what would otherwise be popular commercial programming to include a PSB aspect (for example, providing a broader range of music in a programme series on Classic FM or news in a language such as Urdu appended to news programmes in particular regions). The main attraction of such a proposal is that the funding would be available on a competitive basis.

To a limited extent, a prototype model has been in operation for some time. My report (Veljanovski 1989) for Communa Gàidhlig, funded by the Highland and Islands Board, suggested that publicly funded Gaelic language programmes should be sourced through competitive tender, and bid for by the ITV contractors and the BBC in Scotland. This was accepted by the then Conservative government when it established the Gaelic Broadcasting Committee (Comataidh Craolaidh Gàidhlig) in 1991. Its purpose was to manage the Gaelic Broadcasting Fund of £9.5 million a year in order to support Gaelic language programmes set up under the Broadcasting Act 1990. The Committee was charged with funding up to 200 hours of Gaelic television programmes, and with enhancing and widening the range of Gaelic sound

---

3   The chapter by Tim Congdon later in this book does suggest full privatisation. Indeed, Congdon argues that the size of the BBC is one of the attractions of privatisation, as it would then be able to compete with other media giants in an environment in which media companies need to operate across a range of technical platforms.

programmes, to be broadcast mainly in Scotland. In practice, funded programmes are broadcast by the BBC as well as ITV, although the former had no statutory requirement under the Broadcasting Acts to transmit Gaelic programmes funded by the Gaelic Broadcasting Committee. There were drawbacks with the operation of the Gaelic programming initiative – in the choice of programming and the fact that many were broadcast at unsociable hours.

There are major drawbacks with the arts council for the air proposal. It would interpose yet another public institution between broadcaster and viewer, charged with selecting broadcasting content that would inevitably reflect the preferences and tastes of the committee responsible for allocating funds, rather than those of the viewers. The commercial dynamics of subsidised programming may see it fund unattractive programming shown at inconvenient times. The role of the BBC would also remain unresolved. If the BBC were confined to core PSB services, the arts council for the air proposal may effectively sound its death knell. One cannot have such a body and a protected BBC (and C4).

Conclusion

The market failure framework has never and does not today provide the solid basis for PSB, even within the narrow confines of the paternalistic, programming values espoused by supporters of PSB. The present system is highly distortive and does not achieve the maximum programme diversity; and the BBC is over-reliant on popular programmes for its political support and survival. Furthermore, the ownership and funding of PSB creates an enclave of the broadcasting sector that is largely immune from commercial forces, but which adopts a commercial approach where it is convenient, thus posing unfair competition to the commercial broadcasters.

There is also what might be called the licence fee paradox. The licence fee is perhaps the best way of funding the BBC, should one want a BBC. It creates the best link between viewer and broadcaster (apart from pay-per-view or subscriber services). However, at the same time, it forces the BBC down a populist, commercial route in order to maintain political and popular support for the BBC, making it expand well beyond core PSB programming, and, as a consequence, undermining its *raison d'être*.

But the core issue today is whether, given the pace of technological change and changing viewing habits, two state-owned broadcasters are compatible with a free society and viewer choice. The short answer must be no. The easiest policy to implement would be to privatise C4. A more wide-ranging and sustainable solution policy response must avoid reforming broadcasting in such a way that defines core PSB simply as things that PSBs do. There is a range of policy options. An arts council for the air could be a viable option, but not whilst there is a protected BBC. The BBC could be fully privatised or slimmed down. These options are explored further in later chapters. The status quo is not an option.

References

Altman, W. et al. (1962) *TV: From Monopoly to Competition – and Back?* London: Institute of Economic Affairs.

Beebe, J. (1977) Institutional structure and program choices in television markets. *Quarterly Journal of Economics* 91(1): 15–37.

Caine, S. (1968) *Paying for TV?* London: Institute of Economic Affairs.

Coase, R. H. (1946) The marginal cost controversy. *Economica* 13(51): 169–82.

Coase, R. H. (1947) The origin of the monopoly of broadcasting in Great Britain. *Economica* 14(55): 189–210.

Coase, R. H. (1948) Wire broadcasting in Great Britain. *Economica* 15(59): 194–220.

Coase, R. H. (1950) *British Broadcasting: A Study in Monopoly.* London: Longmans, Green and Co.

Coase, R. H. (1954) The development of the British television service. *Land Economics* 30: 207–22.

Coase, R. H. (1959) The Federal Communications Commission. *Journal of Law and Economics* 2: 1–40.

Coase, R. H. (1960) The problem of social cost. *Journal of Law and Economics* 3: 1–44.

Coase, R. H. (1966) The economics of broadcasting and government policy. *American Economic Review* 56: 440–47.

Coase, R. H. (1974) The market for goods and the market for ideas. *American Economic Review* 64: 384–91.

Davies, G. et al. (1999) The future funding of the BBC – report of the Independent Review Panel. Department for Culture, Media and Sport, July, Her Majesty's Stationery Office.

DCMS (2015) BBC charter review – public consultation. Green Paper, Department for Culture, Media and Sport. https://www.gov.uk/gov ernment/uploads/system/uploads/attachment_data/file/445704/BBC_Charter_Review_Consultation_WEB.pdf

Enders Analysis (2014) How online media services have fulfilled the public service objectives. Public Service Broadcasting Review: 2008–13, 16 December, Ofcom.

European Commission (2002) Press Release I/02/737, 22 May.

Gallagher, R. (1989) American television: fact and fantasy. In *Freedom in Broadcasting* (ed. C. Veljanovski), Chapter 10. London: Institute of Economic Affairs.

House of Lords (2009) Public service broadcasting: short-term crisis, long-term future? Communications Committee, Session 2008–9. www.publications.parliament.uk/pa/ld200809/ldselect/ldcomuni/61/6103.htm#note3

Ofcom (2004) Ofcom review of public service television broadcasting: phase 1, is television special? Consultative Document, 15 June, Ofcom, London, UK.

Ofcom (2005) Ofcom review of public service television broadcasting: Phase 3, Competition for quality. Consultative Document, 8 February, Ofcom, London, UK.

Ofcom (2006) Ofcom review of public service broadcasting. Consultative Document, Ofcom, London, UK.

Ofcom (2007) A new approach to public service content in the digital age: the potential role of the public service publisher. Report, Ofcom, London, UK.

Ofcom (2015a) Public service broadcasting annual report 2015. Report, July, Ofcom, London, UK.

Ofcom (2015b) The communications market report. Report, Office of Communications, Ofcom, London, UK.

Ofcom (2015c) Public service broadcasting in the Internet age. Statement, Ofcom, London, UK.

Owen, B. and Wildman, S. S. (1992) *Video Economics*. Massachusetts, US: Harvard University Press.

Peacock, A. (2004) *Public Service Broadcasting without the BBC?* London: Institute of Economics Affairs.

Peacock Report (1986) *Report of the Committee on Financing the BBC: Cmnd 9824*. Her Majesty's Stationery Office.

Picard, R. G. and Siciliani, P. (eds) (2013) Is there still a place for public service television? Effects of the changing economics of broadcasting. Report, September, Reuters Institute for the Study of Journalism, Oxford University, for the BBC Trust.

Reith, J. (1949) *Into the Wind*. London, UK: Hutchison.

Roberts, D. (1965) *Competition in Radio*. London: Institute of Economic Affairs.

Seabright, P. and von Hagen, J. (eds) (2007) *The Economic Regulation of Broadcasting Markets: Evolving Technology and Challenges for Policy*. Cambridge University Press.

Spence, M. and Owen, B. (1977) Television programming, monopolistic competition, and welfare. *Quarterly Journal of Economics* 91(1): 103–26.

Steiner, P. (1952) Program patterns and preferences, and the workability of competition in broadcasting. *Quarterly Journal of Economics* 66(2): 194–223.

Veljanovski, C. (1987a) Cable and satellite – the market for programmes. Discussion Paper 176, Centre for Economic Policy Research, London, UK.

Veljanovski, C. (1987b) Commercial broadcasting in the UK – over-regulation and mis-regulation. Discussion Paper 175, Centre for Economic Policy Research, London, UK.

Veljanovski, C. (1988a) *Freedom in Broadcasting – Proposal for the Reform of Commercial Television in the UK*. London: Institute of Economic Affairs.

Veljanovski, C. (1988b) Let's switch channels for a better mix. *Sunday Times*, February.

Veljanovski, C. (1989b) Time for a redefined image. *Sunday Times*, May.

Veljanovski, C. (1989c) *The Case for a Gaelic Broadcasting Service*. Inverness: Highlands and Islands Development Board.

Veljanovski, C. (1989d) Public service broadcasting in a competitive era. Paper to BBC Board of Governors, April.

Veljanovski, C. (ed.) (1989e) *Freedom in Broadcasting*. London: Institute of Economic Affairs.

Veljanovski, C. (1990a) Is the media like cheese? In *Law and Welfare Economics* (ed. P. D. Coljee et al.). Amsterdam Free University.

Veljanovski, C. (1990b) Market driven broadcasting: not myth but reality. *Intermedia* 18(6): 17–21.

Veljanovski, C. (1996) Privatisation of Channel 4. Report, European Media Forum, London, UK.

Veljanovski, C. (2000) Is sports broadcasting a public utility? Paper to Seminar 'Sport and Broadcasting', 18 October, Institute of Economic Affairs.

Veljanovski, C. (2001) A market-led information economy. In *Culture and Communications – Perspectives on Broadcasting and the Information Society*. London: Independent Television Commission.

Veljanovski, C. and Bishop, W. D. (1983) *Choice by Cable: The Economics of a New Era in Television*. London: Institute of Economic Affairs.

Veljanovski, C. and Yarrow, G. (1985) *The Effects on ITV and Other Media of Advertising on the BBC*. London: Her Majesty's Stationery Office.

3 THE PROBLEM OF BIAS IN THE BBC

Ryan Bourne

Introduction

The BBC is regularly accused of bias. Over the last decade, there has been sustained criticism of the BBC's coverage of Britain's membership of the EU.[1] Republicans complain that the BBC's coverage of the royal family is too deferential.[2] Independence campaigners in Scotland believe the BBC's referendum coverage was biased towards the union.[3] On the Israel–Palestine conflict,[4] immigration,[5] National Health Service (NHS) reforms[6] and American politics,[7] the BBC has also been criticised. Some

---

1 See extensive list of reports by News-watch: http://news-watch.co.uk/monitoring-projects-and-reports/

2 See the website of Republic: https://republic.org.uk/what-we-do/news-and-updates/bbc-accused-blocking-embarrassing-royal-stories

3 www.theguardian.com/media/2014/jun/02/bbc-scottish-independence-accused-pro-union-bias-good-morning-scotland-gary-robertson

4 At various times, the BBC has been accused of being biased against Israel (www.dailymail.co.uk/debate/article-2193845/Why-wont-BBC-come-clean-bias-Israel--moral-country-deserves-support.html) and in favour of Israel (www.independent.co.uk/news/uk/home-news/hundreds-protest-against-bbc-proisrael-bias-of-gaza-coverage-in-cities-across-the-uk-9609016.html).

5 www.migrationwatchuk.org/press-article/89

6 www.newstatesman.com/blogs/broadcast/2012/10/pro-coalition-bias-bbcs-coverage-nhs-reforms

7 www.spectator.co.uk/features/3276176/the-bbc-cant-help-loving-obama-just-as-it-cant-help-encouraging-recession/

even claim that there are systematic biases in its entertainment programming (Sewell 2012).

However, bias is difficult to measure, and it is, of course, a highly subjective issue. Judging bias requires an understanding of what 'unbiased' or 'neutral' might be. Furthermore, all organisations have inherent biases in the way they operate or present issues, even if they would like to think otherwise. It would, indeed, be surprising if this were not true of the BBC. In this context, it is worth noting that a number of prominent former and current BBC employees have suggested that the BBC 'world-view' exhibits a metropolitan liberal outlook with a bias towards the conventional wisdoms of this world-view. The presenter Andrew Marr, for example, has said the BBC is 'a publicly funded urban organisation with an abnormally large proportion of younger people, of people in ethnic minorities and almost certainly of gay people,' creating 'an innate liberal bias'.[8] Peter Sissons has described a '"mindset" ... a way of thinking firmly of the Left'.[9] Rod Liddle, the former editor of the *Today* programme, has written on the BBC's coverage of the euro that 'the BBC's bias was arrived at through a sort of inherent wet liberalism, rather than an actual plot as such'.[10] More recently, Roger Mosey, a former editorial director, suggested the BBC has a 'liberal-defensive' bias.[11]

The counter to this is sometimes that the BBC exhibits a deep-rooted small 'c' conservatism when it comes to a range of issues such as constitutional coverage of the royal family and the armed forces. But, under an institutional explanation of bias, an innately liberal culture coupled with apparent conservatism on some issues is not directly contradictory. Both are consistent with the view that, institutionally, the BBC might reflect a soft

---

8   http://news.bbc.co.uk/1/hi/entertainment/6764779.stm

9   www.dailymail.co.uk/news/article-1349506/Left-wing-bias-Its-written-BBCs
    -DNA-says-Peter-Sissons.html

10 http://biasedbbc.org/blog/2011/09/24/rod-liddle-explains-bbc-pro-euro-bias/

11 www.thetimes.co.uk/tto/news/uk/article4476635.ece

liberal or progressive but broadly establishment opinion. This hypothesis would suggest that the apparent conservatism on certain issues may mainly be reflective of the BBC's historical role as a national public service broadcaster as well as the selection bias of those who choose to work there given this knowledge.

Unsurprisingly, the BBC itself is extremely defensive about all of these 'accusations'. It seizes on reports that dismiss accusations of 'left-of-centre' bias and uses the fact that it gets criticised from left and right to robustly defend itself against charges of political or ideological favouritism. Yet, few suggest that the BBC is overtly and deliberately biased at all times, particularly towards or against a political party. It is more that an institutional worldview sometimes appears to shape coverage, whether through decisions on what to cover, what to include in a story or what to admit. Just because figures on the left and right sometimes moan about the effects of this world-view does not implicitly make the BBC 'neutral'.

Does bias matter?

Some acknowledge that bias of this kind might be inevitable in any media organisation. It is extremely difficult to provide news that can 'educate and inform' without making judgements that people interpret as 'slant'. Furthermore, some (such as Matthew Taylor from the Royal Society of Arts) believe that commercial news stations might exhibit their own biases, which tend to favour certain market-based viewpoints, meaning the existence of the BBC provides a necessary counterweight.

This is highly doubtful. The extensive, detailed work of Tim Groseclose on the US media market (a more commercial landscape) has comprehensively shown that, while there do exist some media organisations, such as Fox News, which exhibit conservative biases, the overwhelming majority of national news outlets tend to lean to the left in comparison with the views of the general population (Groseclose 2012). He attributes this to the self-selection of journalists being more likely to be 'liberal' (in the American sense of the word) in the first place.

It is certainly not argued in this chapter that the BBC is likely to be more biased than other media organisations. There is no doubt about the difficulties inherent in producing unbiased news. However, there are four key reasons why bias might be particularly important in the context of talking about the future of the BBC.

The first is that the BBC's reputation for fair coverage is much stronger than that of other media organisations. Trust in the BBC is higher than in other media institutions, and it is the largest source of news in the UK. A poll by YouGov found that 31 per cent of the public believe that BBC journalists are most likely to tell the truth, compared with just 17 per cent for ITV news and 15 per cent for the 'upmarket' press.[12] Given the BBC's reach, and the trust placed in it, any biases could potentially have a much more significant impact on altering public understanding of an issue than biases arising on other media platforms.

There is evidence that media bias generally alters public opinion in the US in terms of how people vote (DellaVigna and Kaplan 2007; George and Waldfogel 2006; Gerber et al. 2009). The work of Knight and Chiang (2008) has also shown that the effects of newspaper endorsements are more effective in terms of influencing election results when they are unexpected. This implies that, if a news source has a reputation for bias, it is less able to change people's minds. Given that the biases of other media outlets (particularly newspapers) tend to be better known and more widely acknowledged than those of the BBC, we would expect the BBC to have a much bigger impact on public opinion than other news sources.

---

12 Yougov/London Press Club on Trust: https://d25d2506sfb94s.cloudfront.net/
    cumulus_uploads/document/ea1ioktxin/Results-for-Public-Trust-In-Institutions
    -24112014-W.pdf

Another reason why BBC bias is important is that, unlike its broadcast competitors and newspapers, the BBC is guaranteed its funds through a compulsory licence fee. Consumers are not able to punish the institution financially for perceived coverage bias. This puts it in a highly privileged position, one in which TV viewers are made to pay for the content, irrespective of their views on it.

In addition, the method through which the BBC is funded means that the organisation itself has a vested interest in the political process. It uses a chunk of its guaranteed revenues to lobby for the maintenance of the licence fee. If a government had a manifesto commitment to radically slash or abolish the BBC licence fee, the BBC's coverage of that issue could be vitally important in framing that debate. This is not a mere theoretical point – recently, Andrew Marr interviewed BBC Director General Lord (Tony) Hall on just this issue.[13]

Finally, the BBC has a very high proportion of news content. There would be legitimate competition concerns even if there were no concerns about bias. If it is accepted that any media organisation is likely to exhibit biases, then we should be concerned if there is considerable market power wielded by any news organisation, whether it is in the private or the public sector.

Absolute or relative bias?

Before seeking to measure bias, we first have to outline exactly what we mean by it. In particular, it is important to understand the distinction between *absolute* bias (defined here as a deviation in coverage from objective truth) and *relative* bias (a deviation from the position of another, whether that be public opinion, the views of politicians or some other metric). Absolute bias is difficult to assess, because many of the relevant issues will not relate to questions that are objective by nature.

---

13 www.bbc.co.uk/news/entertainment-arts-33215141

However, when it comes to relative bias, it is highly unlikely that any institution or news source will be totally unbiased. At some stage, editorial decisions must be made on what to cover, who to invite to speak on a subject and how to present the subject. We can assess relative bias more easily than absolute bias (see Groseclose 2012). Whether we are comparing the BBC's coverage with that of other media outlets, or with public opinion, or with some subjective view of what should be covered, there are techniques that can be used to assess what the BBC reports, how it reports things and what it omits.

The rest of this chapter examines case studies in order to assess the relative biases of the BBC. The case studies selected here are, of course, also likely to be reflective of the relative biases of the author. However, I believe that the examples below are indicative of problems of relative bias by omission, selection and presentation, with which fair-minded people can identify.

Bias by omission

'You cannot possibly think that' issues

One potential source of bias is a failure to include an outlook, viewpoint or information within a story or series that might be objectively regarded as being important. This might be because it simply does not cross the editor's mind that the viewpoint or perspective is possible, important or acceptable, or that the information is worthy. This is important because exclusion of a particular viewpoint or opinion on a subject might be expected to shift the 'Overton Window' of what it is politically acceptable to say. This can happen in such a way that a viewpoint becomes entirely eliminated from political discourse except at the margins.

On 19 September 2013, the BBC website ran a 'Viewpoints' piece highlighting different opinions on the new policy of tax-payer-funded school meals for all five-to-seven year olds. The government's own pilot study found no health benefits for the policy and did not assess the opportunity cost of the spending. Yet the viewpoints promoted on the BBC website were limited to those who were happy with the policy, to those who hoped that it would be extended, through to those who were delighted with the policy. There was no perspective from anyone who objected to the policy. This was despite several major think tanks strongly objecting to it in the public domain: objections that were covered elsewhere in the media.[14]

It was only when the omission of this viewpoint was highlighted to the BBC that representatives of the Taxpayers' Alliance and Centre for Policy Studies (CPS) were also asked to submit their thoughts.[15] Had this not been the case, a reader of the story on the BBC website who was not well versed in the broader public debate on this issue would have concluded that there was unanimous public support for the policy. It clearly did not occur to the BBC, until it was pointed out, that it was possible to object to the policy except on the grounds that it did not go far enough.

A frequent viewer of or listener to the BBC sees many examples of this 'relative bias by omission' in terms of the non-interventionist viewpoint being ignored. A recent example of this was the reporting of the government's new measures to try to combat the gender pay gap, through imposing new requirements on large companies. The coverage of the story on the BBC News website contained neither expert economic opinion on the use of crude average gender pay gap figures, nor dissenting opinion on the effectiveness of the policies.[16] This is despite economists being extraordinarily sceptical about the whole 'gender pay gap' concept

---

14 For example, both the *Daily Mail* and the *Guardian* covered the story and objections to the policy. See www.dailymail.co.uk/news/article-2423727/Free-school-meals-child-7--austerity-Britain-afford-Nick-Cleggs-600m-giveaway.html and www.theguardian.com/politics/2013/sep/17/clegg-school-meals-tory-deal.

15 www.bbc.co.uk/news/education-24142901

16 www.bbc.co.uk/news/uk-politics-33515629

as a legitimate policy concern. Other newspapers covering this story, from the *Financial Times* to the *Daily Mail*, solicited opinion from a much wider range of sources.[17,18] The BBC's coverage thus exhibited clear 'bias by omission' of important viewpoints. A more recent example on the same issue came on Equal Pay Day on 9 November, when the Fawcett Society's report asserted that men earn 14.2 per cent more per hour than women, which was reported on BBC Online. This is an official statistic, comparing the mean pay of working full-time men with women. But, crucially, and as other Office for National Statistics (ONS) data show, it does not control for age, occupation type, length of service, closeness to home of the job or interruptions in career, which means it is largely a meaningless comparator. None of this nuance was reported in the BBC article. Instead, the headline 'Women in full-time jobs "work for nothing" until 2016' implies the issue is a huge problem – and the only comment from another source was a supporting one from the Trade Union Congress (TUC).[19]

The next example shows that the BBC is not simply biased against positions that might be described as 'free market'. In the case of immigration, it tends to take a line that is biased in favour of a more free-market position. As explained in the serialisation of former BBC executive Roger Mosey's recent book, one evening the BBC late evening news ran a piece on immigration in a racially diverse part of Britain. The package featured one white, working-class voice, who said he was 'perfectly happy' about immigration in the area. Mosey asked the reporter whether this had in fact been representative of public opinion from his vox pops. The reporter explained that the other people interviewed had been 'fairly rabidly racist' and so could not be used. Thus, there was no

---

17 www.dailymail.co.uk/news/article-3160045/David-Cameron-forces-big-firms
    -publish-gender-pay-gap.html

18 www.ft.com/cms/s/0/3f1dfadc-297a-11e5-acfb-cbd2e1c81cca.html#axzz3frhJ68Zb

19 www.bbc.co.uk/news/business-34764812

voice in the package opposed to immigration to the area, despite widespread concern about immigration levels. The BBC itself has acknowledged it was 'slow to reflect the weight of concern [about immigration] in the wider community' – a conclusion of the BBC-endorsed 'Prebble report'.[20]

Omission of EU withdrawalist voices

Whilst the above examples are interesting, one could easily claim that they are rarities, and that, in most cases, the BBC makes strenuous efforts to include all relevant perspectives. But one area where the BBC has come under sustained criticism is in its coverage of Britain's membership of the EU.

News-watch – a monitoring organisation that tracks flagship news programmes such as Radio 4's *Today* programme – has found that voices in favour of Britain's exit from the EU tend to be under-represented relative to those in favour of continued membership.[21] In this instance, the relative bias against voices in favour of EU exit is exemplified by comparing their coverage with public opinion polling, which shows between a third and half of the public being in favour of EU exit at any given time.[22]

Fresh News-watch analysis commissioned for this chapter has sought to combine all News-watch survey sample data on Radio 4's *Today* programme between March 2004 and June 2015.[23] In the monitored sample, the *Today* programme included 4,275 guest speakers on EU themes. Just 132 of these (3.2 per cent)

---

20 www.bbc.co.uk/bbctrust/our_work/editorial_standards/impartiality/breadth _opinion.html

21 Since 1999, News-watch has tracked more than 6,000 hours of BBC programming and analysed its coverage of EU news and current affairs. A back catalogue of their analysis can be found here: http://news-watch.co.uk/monitoring-projects-and-reports/.

22 See, for example: https://yougov.co.uk/news/2015/02/24/eu-referendum-record-lead/ and YouGov's most recent polling on the subject: http://d25d2506sfb94s.cloudfront .net/cumulus_uploads/document/q32gumm58k/ProspectResults_150602_EU.pdf.

23 A period of 252 weeks, 1,512 individual editions and 4,284 hours of monitoring.

were identifiably in favour of Britain's withdrawal from the EU. Furthermore, 72 per cent of withdrawalist speakers were representatives of the UK Independence Party (UKIP), and over a third (37 per cent) of all withdrawalist contributions were from Nigel Farage alone. Left-leaning withdrawalist voices have accounted for just 0.07 per cent of all EU speakers over this period (three appearances from Labour Party supporters and one representative from the Socialist Labour Party).

In comparison with public opinion, the *Today* programme has exhibited significant bias by omission in terms of excluding the voices of those who believe Britain should leave the EU, particularly non-UKIP voices.

There are two potential explanations for this. The first is that a cultural world-view exists that is broadly pro-EU, and this manifests itself in the omission of strongly anti-EU voices. The second is that the nature of the BBC's position and funding means that it shapes choices on issues through the prism of the political process, rather than public concerns.

Whatever the mechanism, News-watch has examined other case studies that have delivered similar results. In a January 2013 edition of *Newsnight* devoted entirely to David Cameron's announcement of the in/out referendum, one might have expected the debate to be balanced between those favouring 'in' and 'out'. However, Nigel Farage was the lone overt withdrawalist on the show and was set against eighteen other guest speakers who favoured continued membership of the EU.

With a referendum on Britain's membership of the EU scheduled for 23 June 2016, this relative bias by omission could be very important indeed. Within academic media theory, there is a line of reasoning that media influence on audiences is not immediate but occurs more through a continual process of repeated arguments – the 'drip-drip-drip' effect. However, even with the referendum so close, there is still evidence of this bias by omission today.

News-watch's most recent analysis for this chapter examined business views of the EU referendum on the *Today* programme during the official 2015 General Election campaign. During this period, 25 speakers spoke about the subject, of which two gave a neutral response; two (both from the Confederation of British Industry (CBI)) said that the referendum decision was a matter for government, but they were generally pro-EU membership; and two (Conservative politicians) said they were in favour of the referendum but wished to remain in a reformed EU. The remaining nineteen speakers all saw the in/out referendum as a worry or a threat to business.

Certainly, this viewpoint about the impact of the referendum is legitimate. But polling undertaken for Business for Britain and YouGov has found that, in a sample of 1,000 small, medium and large firms, business backed the holding of a referendum by 66 per cent to 25 per cent. It seems reasonable to assume that a substantial proportion of those backing the referendum were doing so in the belief that Britain would be better off economically outside the EU, or at least that the referendum would not be overly damaging for British business. Yet the overwhelming narrative in the selection of guests was that the referendum, by creating uncertainty, would be bad for business and bad for Britain. Audiences on the *Today* programme have been offered no perspective that might suggest that the in/out referendum or leaving the EU is an opportunity for Britain rather than a concern.

Clearly, the future of the UK's position in the EU divides political parties and also the business community. But in its selection of guests, perhaps driven by the state of the political landscape at the time, the *Today* programme has at least exhibited a clear relative bias by omission against a significant strand of opinion. Given the BBC's funding mechanism and reputation, this could have an important impact as the UK prepares to vote in a referendum on membership of the EU.

Bias by selection

A second potential source of bias is 'bias by selection'. This might entail particular issues or viewpoints being more frequently covered, or certain guests or organisations being more likely to be selected. This strand of bias can occur even if a particular journalist does not have a deliberate and overt ideological perspective; they might merely perceive certain stories or viewpoints to be more important or credible due to their own outlook, or because the BBC's role and world-view encourages their coverage.

For example, in the past year there have been many more TV and radio shows dedicated to the subject of inequality on the BBC than, for example, the promotion of economic growth or reducing the deficit. This is despite all three issues being ranked as approximately equally important in surveys of the British public.[24] It is also despite the fact that inequality has been falling on most conventional measures in recent years. Within some of these inequality shows, there was a clear bias in the selection of guests. Jacques Peretti's *The Super-Rich and Us* series, aired on BBC2, was clearly biased in the selection of guest contributors towards those who considered income and wealth inequality to be an extremely important and worrying topic.

Trying to find evidence of bias by selection in any systematic way, though, is incredibly difficult, given the breadth of BBC content. One must restrict analysis to a given narrow range of content to get meaningful results. The author accepts that there might be bias by selection in his own selection. However, the evidence below suggests that there is a strong case to answer.

---

24 http://i100.independent.co.uk/article/this-is-what-the-british-public-actually-care-about--xy-_vOEa9l

Selection of think tanks

The CPS recently published work on the use of think tanks on the BBC website between 1 June 2010 and 31 May 2013. Using the *Guardian* and *Telegraph* newspapers as 'anchors' for the left and right, regression analysis found that the BBC News website's selection of think tanks was much more statistically sensitive to the appearance of that think tank in the *Guardian*, implying a relative bias towards left-leaning content or, at the very least, content more similar to the *Guardian* than the *Telegraph* (Latham 2013).

The CPS methodology was criticised on two grounds when it was released. Firstly, Chris Cook pointed out that journalists often used quotes or analysis from think tanks of different perspectives in their newspaper stories, so that the context of citations matters. Secondly, it was claimed that the *Guardian* is more interested in stories surrounding public services than the *Telegraph*. One might expect the BBC, a public service broadcaster, to also be more likely to cover such stories.

It has been suggested that rather than using newspapers as 'anchors' to test whether the BBC's online coverage leans to the left or right, it would be better to use citations of think tanks in Hansard's record of Parliament. It is suggested that right-leaning think tanks would be more likely to be cited by Conservative MPs and left-leaning think tanks would be more likely to be cited by Labour MPs (a methodology developed by Tim Groseclose in the US). The assumption here is that politicians are more likely to cite think tanks that broadly share their ideological world-view. There is obviously a problem with this approach in that the divides between parties are not as clear as the divides between think tanks, and the positioning of parties is also different from that of think tanks. Of course, it is possible that a member of a party might cite think tanks with views that oppose their own in order to make a point in a debate that his or her opponents' views are criticised by think tanks that would be expected to be friendly to his or her party.

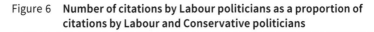

Figure 6   Number of citations by Labour politicians as a proportion of citations by Labour and Conservative politicians

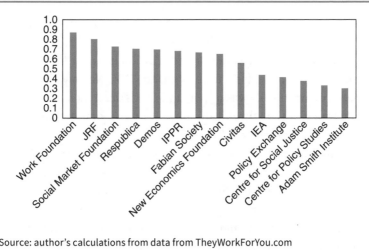

Source: author's calculations from data from TheyWorkForYou.com

The author selected fourteen multidisciplinary think tanks from across the political spectrum that have had 20 or more Parliamentary citations (Lords and the Commons) amongst Conservative and Labour politicians between the 2010 and 2015 elections. The think tanks are ranked from the most left wing by this metric in Figure 6. In fact, the results generally accord with intuition regarding which think tanks we would expect to be the most left-leaning, with the possible exception of the New Economics Foundation.

As can be seen in Table 2, there is no evidence of correlation between the tendency for the BBC to select left-leaning think tanks as left-leaning is defined above.[25] This suggests that either

25 This searching was undertaken using the website TheyWorkForYou.com. All individual citations were counted, irrespective of whether they came from the same speaker or the same debate. Likewise, citations in written questions were counted too, except in instances where the think tank citation appears in Parliamentary questions repeated to many different Secretaries of State and ministers.

Table 2   **Think-tank citations by politicians and the BBC News website**

Think tank	Labour mentions	Conservative mentions	Relative Labour mentions	BBC mentions
Work Foundation	21	3	0.88	55
Joseph Rowntree Foundation	161	39	0.81	110
Social Market Foundation	21	8	0.72	18
Respublica	17	7	0.71	16
Demos	46	20	0.70	85
IPPR	106	49	0.68	104
Fabian Society	14	7	0.67	37
New Economics Foundation	19	10	0.66	39
Civitas	14	11	0.56	40
IEA	19	24	0.44	104
Policy Exchange	34	47	0.42	139
Centre for Social Justice	62	103	0.38	82
Centre for Policy Studies	16	32	0.33	33
Adam Smith Institute	6	14	0.30	37
Correlation between relative Labour mentions and BBC mentions				−0.1

Source: politician citations from TheyWorkForYou.com. BBC News website mentions using targeted Google search

the BBC exhibits no relative biases in its selection of think tanks, or that any biases that do occur are contextual. Nevertheless, the data seem to suggest no systematic 'bias by selection' here.

One possibility, though, is that there might still be relative bias in selection in terms of the *types* of stories in which different think tanks are cited. The research also reviewed all of the 410 BBC media hits that the IEA received in a twelve-month period between July 2014 and June 2015, from appearances on broadcast through to mentions on the BBC website.

It is notable that, out of those 410 mentions, the IEA was not asked to comment or was quoted once on immigration by the BBC, despite the clear classical liberal position of IEA authors and senior staff on this topic. We were also quoted on poverty only once, despite having published two major research papers by Dr Kristian Niemietz in recent years, which have been widely discussed in the print media and highly regarded by think tanks of all shades of opinion.

How can a free-market think tank get so much coverage on welfare but not on poverty (on which we have done far more extensive work)? And how can it be that a classical liberal organisation has received no coverage on immigration in a twelve-month period, despite its prominence as an issue?

One potential explanation is that the editorial teams of many BBC programmes have clear priors about the world-view associated with the staff of a free-market think tank, predicated along some left–right dichotomy. Since 'free-market' economics is associated in the UK more with the 'right' of the political spectrum than the 'left', many journalists project other perceived 'right' opinions onto free-market think tanks. For example, there is a range of opinion that assumes that the 'right' does not care about the poor, which might explain why we rarely get asked to discuss poverty. It is also perceived that right-leaning people are opposed to immigration. Over the past few years, there have been several occasions when the IEA communications team has received calls from BBC journalists who have assumed that an IEA spokesperson will be opposed to free movement of people within the EU.

It should be noted that such inherent biases will also apply to certain think tanks on the left, though perhaps more on social issues than on economic issues. It might be assumed, for example, that a left-leaning organisation will have socially liberal views on the role of the state in relation to sexual matters, or will be in favour of Britain remaining in the EU.

Thought for the Day

One area where a BBC show has editorial control over the selection of guests is on the Radio 4 *Today* programme slot *Thought for the Day*. *Thought for the Day* is broadcast each morning (Monday to Saturday) at around 7.50 a.m. and entails a scripted monologue of around three minutes in length from an invited speaker. The slot aims to deliver 'reflections from a faith perspective on issues and people in the news'. The theme is selected by the invited commentator and compiled under the auspices of the Manchester-based BBC Religion and Ethics department, separate from *Today*'s editorial team.

Research undertaken by News-watch surveyed all editions of *Thought for the Day* available within the BBC online archive to assess how issues related to economics and business are discussed. This allows us to make an assessment of whether there is evidence of some form of anti-capitalist or anti-market bias by selection for the slot.

Our overall sample was 976 separate editions. Of these, 167 (17 per cent) included discussion of economics, business, finance and matters of public policy necessitating economic policy judgements.

This sample was then coded according to whether the speaker offered a positive, negative or neutral/factual/mixed perspective on market-based and capitalist activity within the issue under discussion. The coding frame was set such that positive opinions incorporated those extolling the virtues of business activity or capitalists, the importance of economic growth and economic freedom and the improvements in living standards seen under capitalism. Negative opinions included those that denounced market-based activities, highlighted negative examples of business activity, questioned the morality of capitalism and/or demanded significant interventions or controls on voluntary activity and exchange. All other contributions fell under the neutral, factual or mixed heading.

An important point to highlight with the negative opinions is that these often contained denouncement of genuinely corrupt activities – not things that those believing in a free economy would seek to defend. They are counted as negative here, though, because the continued highlighting of negative stories in relation to business is seldom balanced with positive stories (such as private companies delivering high-quality education in the developing world, for example). The selection of stories therefore contributes to a climate in which business and market-based activity is heavily associated with cronyism and corruption.

The results of this analysis are striking. Of the 167 editions analysed, 109 (65 per cent) expressed a negative opinion; 45 (27 per cent) were neutral, factual or mixed, and only 13 (8 per cent) gave any sort of positive perspective on the theme. As such, negative commentary outweighed positive commentary by a factor of more than eight to one.[26]

In the relatively small number of editions that could be regarded as positive towards pro-market or capitalist positions, it was noted that businesses could achieve good outcomes, that businessmen were capable of acts of giving, insight and philanthropy and that such efforts could be valuable to communities. But these were vastly outweighed by what might be described as a plethora of anti-market or anti-capitalist opinions.

---

26 The full results of this exercise, along with key quotes from each edition and commentary as to why particular coding decisions were made, are available from the author.

- Several contributors denounced multinational corporations and the plutocrats who now selfishly own so much of the world's wealth.
- The vulnerabilities of the poor were highlighted as if capitalism caused poverty, but the role of capitalism in alleviating poverty was barely mentioned.
- Cuts to government spending in areas such as welfare and health were focused on regularly, but without corresponding attention being given to problems such as dependency or the strains placed on provision due to an ageing population.
- Economic growth – the driver of improved living standards – was opposed and downplayed, whilst several contributors attacked the straw man idea that politicians seek to maximise GDP.[27]
- Free-market ideology was attacked – with crude denouncements of neoliberalism, Ayn Rand and the idea of 'trickle down' economics – even though there is no real evidence of any prominent free-market economist ever advocating the latter.[28]
- The issue of tax avoidance was discussed in moral terms, implying it was inherently moral for corporations to pay more tax than was legally due. No contributor suggested politicians had the power to change tax law.
- In several instances, capitalist activities were said to lead to 'exploitation'. The existence of sweat shops was lamented, without ever discussing the likely negative impact the non-existence of these industries would have in developing countries.[29]

---

27 www.iea.org.uk/sites/default/files/publications/files/Selfishness,%20Greed%20 and%20Capitalism.pdf, p. 37.

28 www.iea.org.uk/blog/forget-trickle-down-in-a-free-market-the-rich-don %E2%80%99t-gain-at-the-poor%E2%80%99s-expense

29 www.iea.org.uk/blog/sweat-shops-and-the-need-for-libertarian-moral-outrage

- Inequality was regularly held up as being self-evidently a huge problem, with highly contentious figures from Oxfam and others cited. At no point was it pointed out that global inequality was falling.[30]
- The financial crash and illegal activities of banks and financial entities were regularly discussed, but nothing was said about the role of government policies, including regulatory and monetary failure, in contributing to these outcomes.
- Markets and business were said to be eroding moral values. Investors in art (from the 'jet set and hedge funds'), for example, were concerned only in the value of the paintings and had no sense of aesthetics. Anti-consumerism and a dislike of advertising pervaded several contributions.
- Scandals in certain sectors and businesses – G4S, Libor, UBS, Findus Foods, etc. – were used to justify wholesale reforms to business policy.
- New technologies such as Bitcoin and smartphones were denounced, with rare exposition of the benefits of these new technologies to people's lives.
- Speakers frequently advocated the need for ambitious action to combat climate change. Strikingly, whilst the human cost of climate change was mentioned, there was no discussion of the cost to the global poor of mitigation policies.

While one might expect religious leaders to focus on certain topics – such as the conditions of the poor, inequality, business morality and the common good – this need not necessitate such stringent anti-market views as seen from the large sample examined. There is a clear bias in selection here against opinions that hold business, capitalism and economic activity not

---

30 http://blogs.spectator.co.uk/coffeehouse/2015/01/beware-oxfams-dodgy
    -statistics-on-wealth-inequality/

centrally planned by governments in a positive light. *Thought for the Day*, in its discussion of economic issues at least, overwhelmingly represents a world-view that, at best, is sceptical of capitalism and voluntary market-based exchange, and, at worst, disdains it.

Bias by presentation

Perhaps the most difficult form of relative bias to measure is 'bias by presentation'. This entails examining the context around how stories and participants are presented as well as how opinions are introduced – and whether this means the audience is nudged towards believing that one subjective viewpoint is right or more credible.

Value judgements

An obvious example is the use of value judgements in presenting a story. One that immediately springs to mind is the way that BBC journalist Norman Smith covered the 2014 Autumn Statement, reporting that the OBR had forecast that spending levels as a proportion of GDP would likely fall to levels last seen in the late 1930s. Rather than just outlining this fact, the presentation of the story by Smith entailed substantial value judgements about what this would mean (my emphasis in italics):

> when you sit down and read the Office for Budget Responsibility report it reads like a *book of doom*. It is *utterly terrifying*, suggesting that spending will have to be *hacked back* to the levels of the 1930s as a proportion of GDP. That is *an extraordinary concept*, you're back to the land of *Road to Wigan Pier*.[31]

---

31 www.telegraph.co.uk/news/politics/david-cameron/11272814/PM-attacks-BBC
    -over-Wigan-Pier-cuts-coverage.html

The OBR figures have since been strongly criticised as being misleading in terms of historical comparisons.[32] For example, real GDP (and therefore spending) is much higher; the figures used different measures of GDP, which makes an enormous difference in the comparisons; and there were vastly different sums spent on defence and debt interest in the 1930s (and by implication the residual on items such as health and education).

But, even if the figures had been directly comparable, would state spending at 35 per cent of GDP be so 'terrifying'? Is it really terrifying for the state in the UK to spend the same proportion of national income as the state in other developed countries, such as Australia, Switzerland and South Korea? Making this comparison led to weeks of media coverage with this claim being repeated.

Sometimes descriptions are more systematically misleading. For example, in recent years there has been a proliferation of stories about tax avoidance, often involving large companies such as Amazon, Starbucks and Google. Yet in 24 of the 78 stories on the BBC website between 2012 and 2015 that mentioned 'Amazon' and 'tax avoidance', corporation tax paid by companies was misleadingly compared with sales revenues – which has nothing to do with the tax base for corporation tax that is profit.[33] As it happens, these cases are all much more complicated in other ways, but the comparison of corporation tax paid with sales is meaningless and clearly designed to influence the reputations of those companies and views on tax avoidance.[34]

---

32 www.iea.org.uk/blog/is-george-osborne-really-returning-us-to-a-1930s-govern ment-accurate-comparisons-suggest-a-defi

33 Author's calculation from Google search of BBC website between 2012 and 2015 for 'Amazon' and 'tax avoidance'.

34 This was an example first raised by my colleague, Philip Booth: www.iea.org.uk/ blog/bbc-corporation-tax-horror-story.

Health warnings

Perhaps the most egregious example of this relative bias by presentation came back in March 2012, when the subject of minimum alcohol pricing was under discussion. BBC2's *Newsnight* had organised a debate to take place on the subject between Eric Joyce (an MP opposed to the proposal) and Sarah Wollaston MP (who was in favour), chaired by Emily Maitlis.[35] Wollaston was introduced as 'a GP and a Tory MP, not to mention a member of the Commons' Health Select Committee'. The introduction for her opponent was: 'Eric Joyce, an MP against minimum pricing, was forced to quit the Labour Party after a drunken punch-up in the House of Commons bar. Tonight he's under curfew in his Edinburgh home.' The way that this was introduced clearly would leave viewers uninitiated in the subject to simply assume that Wollaston had a monopoly on credibility to talk about the issue, even though both MPs were on the show to assess the economic and political implications of the policy, as well as the health effects.

Though not as overt as this, it is common for BBC coverage to attach 'health warnings' to participants in debates. In the context of a discussion, unbalanced introductions act to undermine the credibility of one of the speakers, or enhance the credibility of the other.

Academic economists have noted how a common form of media bias involves putting 'an ideological label on conservative and libertarian organisations and interviewees, but not on liberal and leftist groups' (Boaz 2010). This sort of 'bias by presentation' is commonplace on the BBC.

Building on CPS research (Latham 2013), the treatment of fifteen multidisciplinary think tanks on the BBC news website was analysed between the general elections in 2010 and 2015. All

---

35 See http://velvetgloveironfist.blogspot.co.uk/2012/03/entirely-matter-for-you
.html for details.

articles containing the names of the think tanks were examined to ascertain whether health warnings had been used to describe the organisations.[36] 'Health warnings' here, as with Latham's analysis, include: (a) a statement of the ideological or political position of the think tank, (b) an expression of the think tank's prior position on an issue or (c) mention of an affiliation of any political actor to the think tank. The results are presented in Table 3.

As can be seen, think tanks perceived to be conservative or free market are much more likely to be ascribed a health warning. The four main think tanks that advocate for free-market policies are given ideological warning labels including 'free market', 'centre–right' and 'right-wing' often: the IEA 22.1 per cent of the time, the CPS 30.3 per cent of the time, Policy Exchange 41.7 per cent of the time and the Adam Smith Institute 59.5 per cent of the time. The communitarian conservative Respublica is given an ideological warning label 50 per cent of the time.

In contrast, left-leaning think tanks are given these labels far less often. The New Economics Foundation is probably the most left-leaning policy think tank in the country, and its output lies further from mainstream opinion than any other.[37] Yet the only health warnings it has been ascribed are, in effect, compliments – it was described as a 'sustainability think tank' and a 'member of the Tescopoly alliance'. Demos and the Institute for Public Policy Research (IPPR), despite having clear ideological left-leaning positions, are introduced as such much less often than their equivalents at Policy Exchange or the Centre for Policy Studies.

---

36 The think tanks used were: the Work Foundation, the New Economics Foundation, the Social Market Foundation, Demos, the Joseph Rowntree Foundation, Civitas, the Institute for Public Policy Research (IPPR), the IEA, the CPS, the Centre for Social Justice, Policy Exchange, the Fabian Society, Respublica and the Adam Smith Institute.

37 Its policy recommendations, for example, have recently included simply reducing the length of the working week: www.neweconomics.org/blog/entry/reduce-the-working-week-to-30-hours.

Health warnings such as 'centre-left' or 'centre-right' are used to inform the readers that a think tank or organisation might be seeking to shift public opinion in a particular direction. Therefore, we might expect that think tanks with close associations or formal relationships with political parties would be more likely to be assigned ideological warning labels. Thus, it is unsurprising that the Fabian Society receives health warnings a very large proportion of the time, since it is actually affiliated with the Labour Party. Likewise, the Centre for Policy Studies has strong political associations with the Conservative Party. There is a greyer area as far as the Centre for Social Justice and Policy Exchange are concerned. They are independent of the Conservative Party, but there is no question that there is regular exchange of personnel and ideas between those groups and the government. The situation is very similar to that which existed between the IPPR and the Labour Party. However, the IPPR was given health warnings on about one-sixth of appearances, the Centre for Social Justice on about one-third and Policy Exchange on over 40 per cent of the occasions on which they appeared.

This, therefore, seems like a clear relative bias. The BBC News website is much more likely to use ideological or political labels when introducing right-of-centre or free-market opinion. It could be that because they think left-leaning think tanks are more credible, do better research or – most likely – because these think tanks are closer to their own world-view, they do not even notice the relative positions of these think tanks.

Sometimes, the BBC uses positive adjectives to describe think tanks, such as 'independent': the Institute for Fiscal Studies (IFS) is often given this label. As the final two columns of Table 3 show, sometimes other think tanks are given this label too. That this adjective is so rarely used makes it a powerful, positive signal that the viewpoint should be taken seriously and is untainted by political biases.

Table 3   **Think-tank mentions and health warnings on the BBC website in the previous Parliament**

Think tank	BBC mentions	% of mentions with health warnings	Health warnings	% of mentions with positive adjectives	Positive adjectives
Work Foundation	55	0.0		3.6	'a not-for-profit body', 'an independent body'
New Economics Foundation	39	5.1	'member of Tescopoly Alliance', 'sustainability think tank'	7.7	'independent think tank'
Social Market Foundation	18	5.6	'left-of-centre think tank'	0.0	
Demos	85	11.8	'left-leaning think tank', 'political think tank', 'centre-left think tank', 'left-wing think tank', 'left-leaning think tank', 'centre-left research organisation'	7.1	'independent', 'independent political researchers', 'cross-party think tank'
Joseph Rowntree Foundation	110	13.6	'anti-poverty think tank', 'social policy charity', 'social justice charity', 'researched poverty', 'anti-poverty charity', 'social chairty', 'social policy research chairty', 'social equality pressure group'	0.0	
Civitas	40	15.0	'right-leaning', 'think-tank interested in limited government and personal freedom'	10.0	'independent think tank'

Continued

Think tank	BBC mentions	% of mentions with health warnings	Health warnings	% of mentions with positive adjectives	Positive adjectives
IPPR	104	16.3	'centre-left think tank', 'a left-of-centre think tank', 'left-leaning'	0.0	
IEA	104	22.1	'right-wing think tank', 'free-market think tank', 'arguably the most vocal think tank opposed to HS2', 'right-leaning think tank', 'centre-right'	0.0	
CPS	33	30.3	'founded by Margaret Thatcher', 'right-wing', 'free-market', 'former Conservative party chairman', 'pro-free market', 'centre-right'	0.0	
Centre for Social Justice	82	32.9	'set up by the Conservative MP Iain Duncan Smith', 'right-leaning think tank', 'Conservative-leaning think tank', 'right-wing think tank', 'a think tank which helped shape the Tories' manifesto'	6.1	'independent'
Policy Exchange	139	41.7	'centre-right think tank', 'right-wing think tank', 'right-leaning think tank', 'Conservative think tank', 'think tank on the right', 'right-of-centre', 'centre-right research organisation', 'government backed think tank' 'petri dish of ideas for the Conservative leadership', 'pro-free market', 'political think tank'	0.0	

Continued

Think tank	BBC mentions	% of mentions with health warnings	Health warnings	% of mentions with positive adjectives	Positive adjectives
Fabian Society	37	45.9	'left-of-centre', 'Labour-supporting', 'left-wing', 'affiliated to the Labour party', 'socialist', 'centre-left', 'left-leaning', 'Labour-leaning'	0.0	
Respublica	16	50.0	'centre-right think tank', 'concept of "Red Tory"', 'Mr Cameron's favourite', 'right-leaning', 'centre-right'	0.0	
Adam Smith Institute	37	59.5	'free market think tank', 'pro-free market think tank', 'free market economics think tank', 'right-wing think tank', 'known for its work on privatisation', 'argues for smaller government and lower taxes', 'a favourite of Margaret Thatcher'	2.7	'independent'

Source: author's targeted Google search of BBC News website

This adjective, however, simply raises the question, 'independent of what?' The IFS has received funding from the Joseph Rowntree Foundation, which has, in turn, been described as a 'pressure group' by the BBC. The author does not for a moment question the academic integrity or very scholarly nature of the work of the IFS. However, this example shows the subjectivity that perhaps lies behind the adjective 'independent'. All of the think tanks in Table 3 (with the exception of the Labour-affiliated Fabian

Society) are 'independent' of political parties, operating separately from them. But few are ever labelled 'independent'. What makes the IFS more independent than, say, Respublica? It would be worth the BBC clarifying in writing exactly what they mean when they use the 'independent' label.

Interruptions

Another way in which bias can manifest itself is through interviews and how they are conducted – for example, the degree of hostility of the interviewer. It is likely that interviewers are more instinctively hostile to those whose views they disagree with or find alien, meaning that a broad sociological bias can lead to some interviewees being treated differently if they fall outside a particular world-view.

News-watch analysis of the EU debate has in the past found that eurosceptic voices are interrupted, for example, far more often than pro-European politicians.[38] More recently, in a case study example, News-watch showed two interviews in its Winter 2013 Survey, highlighting how pro-European and eurosceptic voices were treated differently in similar length interviews with the same interviewer. On 18 November 2013, Paul Sykes, a UKIP donor, was interviewed by Evan Davis on the *Today* programme. The conversation switched between them 60 times (approximately eleven times per minute). In contrast, Davis interviewing Karel De Gucht, a European Trade Commissioner, saw the conversation switch just ten times (twice per minute). This is shown in Figure 7. The word count for the De Gucht interview was also much slower, suggesting that, as well as facing fewer interruptions, the Commissioner was able to make his point in a more relaxed or measured way. Of course, a single case study does not make

---

38 http://news-watch.co.uk/wp-content/uploads/2015/07/Today-Programme
-Survey-Summer-20061.pdf

the point unequivocally. There might be other occasions when the eurosceptic interviewee had a relatively free ride. However, as noted above, earlier research suggests that this case study is representative of a general problem.

Conclusion

Bias is difficult to measure systematically. The BBC has been accused of being biased towards liberal establishment opinion in the past, and there is evidence across a range of case studies consistent with this sort of sociological and institutional explanation.

Biases by omission, selection and presentation (assessed through examination of the context of stories) are the three main ways in which biases manifest themselves. This under-representation of certain viewpoints and slant in selection and presentation is unlikely to be deliberate and decreed from on high; it is more reflective of the underlying beliefs of the BBC journalists, and the structures within which they operate – arising in ways that the journalists themselves might not even consider biased.

The question remains: what are the policy responses? It is not argued that other sources of news and comment are not biased. Commercial news sources, sources financed by charitable trusts and other forms of voluntary news and comment provision (for example, blogs) also have biases. There is no evidence that such sources tend to have a disproportionate pro-free-market or even pro-commerce bias, though some do. In the UK, there is a range of views expressed in the print media, in blogs and in broadcast media and the arts, which are funded from a variety of sources. A range of media, some of which present objective facts and others that offer news and comment from a variety of perspectives is healthy.

However, the position of the BBC is problematic for several reasons.

Figure 7 **EU interview comparisons**

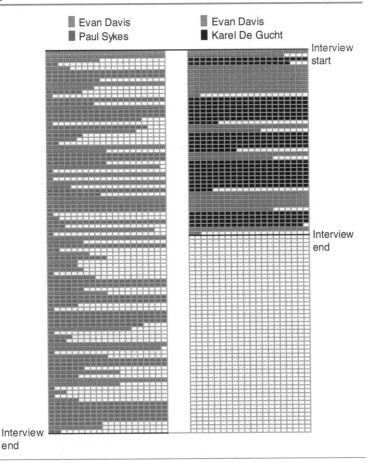

The BBC has a huge share of the news and comment market, the size of which would lead to serious competition concerns if the BBC were a private organisation; in other words, it receives privileged treatment in this respect.[39] The BBC is the biggest provider of

39 The BBC has a privileged position in the proper sense of the word – there are special rules (or exemptions from rules) that do not apply to other organisations.

news on every platform on which it has a presence. Approximately 75 per cent of television news watched in the UK is provided by the BBC, and measures of market power for radio news are around the same. The BBC has somewhat less – though still considerable – market power in online news (see Ofcom 2014).

Furthermore, it should not be possible for an organisation to exercise such market power in an area as subjective as news provision when those who fund the organisation have no choice in the matter. In addition, the fact that the BBC is trusted means that its bias is more influential. As has been noted, the BBC also has an interest in the political process and is happy to use licence-payer funds to promote its cause.

Privatisation would not lead to or guarantee the elimination of relative biases from coverage; the work of Tim Groseclose on the US shows this is extraordinarily unlikely. However, privatisation could lead to change over time and a more sceptical viewing public. Most importantly of all, however, privatisation gives the right of exit to those who do not wish to listen to the programmes broadcast by the BBC. If the normal competition rules applied to the BBC, there would also be a greater plurality of positions. Broadcasters with different biases could compete.

Despite the case made in this chapter, there is no doubt that the BBC has a reputation – generally well deserved – for high quality and broad news coverage, for which it is respected. A privatised BBC would bear a considerable commercial cost if this reputation were impaired; thus, there would be an incentive to maintain it. This is especially true if we consider the worldwide reputation of the BBC and the ability it would have as a private entity to expand its broadcasting reach outside the UK.

References

Boaz, D. (2010) Ideological warning labels. Blog Post, 17 August, Cato @ Liberty.

Dellavigna, S. and Kaplan, E. (2007) The Fox News effect: media bias and voting. *Quarterly Journal of Economics* 122(3): 1187–234.

George, L. and Waldfogel, J. (2006) The *New York Times* and the market for local newspapers. *American Economic Review* 96(15): 435–47.

Gerber, A., Karlan, D. and Bergan, D. (2009) Does the media matter? A field experiment measuring the effect of newspapers on voting behavior and political opinions. *American Economic Journal: Applied Economics* 1(2): 35–52.

Groseclose, T. (2012) *Left Turn: How Liberal Media Bias Distorts the American Mind*. New York: St Martin's Griffin.

Knight, B. and Chiang, C.-F. (2008) Media bias and influence: evidence from newspaper endorsements. Working Paper 14445, National Bureau of Economic Research.

Latham, O. (2013) Bias at the Beeb? A quantitative study of slant in BBC online reporting. Report, Centre for Policy Studies, London.

Ofcom (2014) News consumption in the UK: 2014 report. Report, June, Ofcom, London, UK.

Sewell, D. (2012) *A Question of Attitude: The BBC and Bias Beyond News*. London: The New Culture Forum.

4 WHY IS THE BBC BIASED?

Stephen Davies

Is the BBC biased to the left?

Complaints that the output of the BBC is biased towards a particular perspective or against identifiable positions and views are longstanding, with much argument from figures such as Norman Tebbit to that effect in the 1980s. Interestingly, such arguments come from many parts of the political palette, with Owen Jones recently arguing the exact mirror image of the case made years ago by Tebbit (Jones 2014). Most of the work that has been done on bias in the media has looked at a bias in a particular political direction, with most studies focusing on the US. These use various methodologies to argue that electronic and other media have a pronounced bias towards the liberal side of US politics in a way that makes the output of the media markedly out of line with the views of a large part, or even the majority, of the population (Groseclose 2012). There have been studies of political bias of this kind in the UK as well, and some of the other chapters in this collection make a similar case.

Why, though, should the BBC display a bias or tilt of this kind, if indeed it does so? There are many explanations that amount to conspiracy theories of one kind or another, but these all fall foul of the basic problem of being untestable and assuming a degree of coordination and conscious intention that simply is not revealed by any serious investigation. Moreover, whereas in the US most of the studies show the media in that country as having a clear tilt to the liberal rather than the conservative side, the studies done in the UK are as likely to argue that the BBC has a bias to the right as one to the left (Latham 2013; Wahl-Jorgensen et al. 2012). Not surprisingly, BBC insiders and supporters take this as evidence that the BBC is actually broadly neutral or impartial. If it is annoying left and right in equal measure, surely it must be broadly on the right lines?

However, things are not that straightforward, and the BBC does indeed have a clear bias. This, however, is not a matter of a leaning towards one side or the other of the political spectrum, much less a favouring of one party over another. Instead, the BBC has a bias in favour of what is a clear position, but one that is going to displease many on both the left and the right (though for different reasons, of course). It is also important to realise that this bias is as much a matter of sympathy for a certain type or style of argument as towards any kind of explicit content; but the favouring of that kind of argument will inevitably lead to some positions and views being given greater prominence and others less. It is also important to realise that having a position that upsets in different ways both left and right does not mean that it is therefore 'centrist' or 'moderate'. Rather, it is a view of the world that is distinctive and, because of the BBC's reach, very influential in public discourse. However, it is not simply a product of splitting the difference or 'triangulation'.

Institutional bias and the BBC

The crucial point is that the bias of the BBC is an institutional or systemic bias. That is, it derives from the nature of the institution, its basic procedures and the composition of its staff, rather than from overt policy or political views, however strongly held. To some extent, it derives from the nature of television as a medium and is therefore shared with other broadcasters everywhere. But it also derives primarily from a number of factors that are peculiar to the BBC. Some of these can be changed by reform or managerial decisions, but others cannot, unless the BBC becomes a fundamentally different kind of institution from the one that it now is.

The concept of institutional bias is one that comes originally from organisational theory: in other words, from management studies (for an economist's use of the concept in a wider context, see Eterovic 2011). Much of the work is actually concerned with the various undesirable results this can have in business, such as bullying or poor service delivery. Institutional bias is the way that a process or institution always tends to produce a certain pattern of outcome in a given area, despite there being no conscious or deliberate intention to do so. In fact, there may even be a conscious effort to not produce the biased outcome. The *Oxford Dictionary of Communication* defines the phenomenon as (Chandler and Munday 2011):

> a tendency for the procedures and practices of particular institutions to operate in ways which result in certain social groups being advantaged or favoured and others being disadvantaged or devalued. This need not be the result of any conscious prejudice or discrimination but rather of the majority simply following existing rules or norms.

As the entry goes on to state, the commonest use of the concept is to explain structural disadvantages faced by ethnic or religious groups or a particular sex (which can be men as often as women). Here, we can use the notion to explain why certain kinds of ideological persuasion and also certain identifiable social groups will face disadvantage in terms of their views and circumstances being slighted, ignored or even misrepresented by the BBC. Interestingly, this analysis has some similarities with the so-called propaganda model of US media developed by Chomsky and Herman, although in this case it does not generate the policy conclusions that they draw (Chomsky and Herman 2002).

The argument is that, as the kind of institution it is now, the BBC has an institutional bias towards a certain kind of programme content and presentation, regardless of the views of its staff. The procedures and structures of the BBC lead to a certain way of thinking that permeates current affairs and also much of the cultural and artistic output of the organisation. There is a predominant outlook and content that can be described in various ways. Sympathetic observers might use terms such as 'sensible', 'middle of the road', 'respectable', 'centrist' or 'moderate'. Less friendly accounts might use terms such as 'elitist', 'metropolitan', 'managerialist' or 'conventional'. What we have is a passionate commitment to a received wisdom, rather than a tilt to the left or right in any commonly understood sense of those terms. But whose received wisdom, and how does this arise?

Shared values of BBC staff

The initial factor is the very narrow and restricted background of BBC staff, both of presenters and producers. The proportion who are privately educated (and, by extension, upper-middle class) is several times the national average (Milburn 2014). Generally, they come from professional backgrounds rather than commerce or business, much less from working-class households. Much of the critical comment on the narrow base from which the BBC draws its senior staff emphasises the lack of ethnic or gender diversity; but, while there is undoubtedly something to this, it is swamped by the social origins phenomenon. The women and ethnic minorities who do work for the BBC in roles such as producer, presenter and senior manager are also likely to come from the same kind of educational and social background as their white, male colleagues.

What this naturally leads to is a common shared set of beliefs and attitudes, deriving from common or shared experience. In a very real sense, the conventional wisdom referred to earlier is the shared outlook of a specific social group or formation. The problem, of course, is that, in the absence of challenges or dissent from people from a different background, all kinds of beliefs remain unquestioned, with the status of 'obvious truth' or 'common sense' attached to them. These kinds of unexamined assumptions exist at the level of general principles rather than particular issues. Examples might be that it is always good to help the less fortunate, or that most social problems should be understood as having structural causes rather than being explicable through individual agency and action, or that business activity is a zero-sum game. Moreover, once a particular set of attitudes becomes widely shared within any organisation, it tends to attract people who share them, and so the situation becomes self-perpetuating and reinforcing. As managers in companies all over the world have discovered, changing the culture of an organisation once it has become established is extremely difficult (Denning 2011).

Given both the shared social background of so many staff and the common economic interests that they have by virtue of working for an organisation with the specific status and position of the BBC, there is actually a case for seeing the shared outlook and attitudes as an ideology in the strict sense of the word. In other words, BBC employees form a structured way of perceiving the world that appears to be neutral and objective to those who have it, but which in fact incorporates various self-interested presumptions and helps to justify them. In this case, the ideology in question is that of the professional and managerial class, which places a high value on expertise and the ability of qualified people to both understand and direct complex social processes. This comes with the corollary that undesirable social phenomena are 'problems' that can be resolved, given the correct insight and actions (Harold Perkin

(1990), who identified this particular set of beliefs, preferred to use the term 'class ideal', which conveys the same idea but without the baggage of the term ideology).

Public service role and institutional bias

However, this kind of sociological explanation is not enough and makes the problem appear less intractable than it actually is. The implication is that, with enough change in recruitment at the level of senior management, a cultural revolution in assumptions and attitudes might be brought about. In reality, the nature of the BBC since its foundation in terms of its structures and funding and mission mean that anyone working there will be led to advance a particular way of thinking, even if inadvertently and against their desires.

The first and basic problem is the very concept of a public service broadcaster. This assumes that, left to itself, a purely private television and radio broadcaster will not produce certain kinds of service that are thought to be essential or highly valuable (by a cultural elite at least). This can be presented as a 'market failure', but the underlying presumption is more than that. It is that, in the absence of a broadcaster with a non-market-driven funding base, there will not be enough popular demand for programmes of the 'requisite quality'. In particular, there will not be enough high-quality news and current affairs, because neither the viewing public nor private actors such as investors and advertisers want them enough or have an incentive to provide them. In other words, there is a structural failure of public taste and sentiment and of private provision. This means that an idea of elevating the public consciousness and guiding it, rather than reflecting and articulating it and perhaps helping it to develop, is central to the mission and purpose of the BBC. Despite what is often said, this remains the case, even if the idea of what it means to elevate has changed since Reith's day.

One solution to this supposed problem, adopted in many countries, is to have the government ultimately decide what kind of elevating programming a state-funded broadcaster should put out. For good and obvious reasons, this option was not taken, and instead the model of the licence fee was used. There is still, though, the underlying idea of an educative and enlightening mission, and the content of that has to come from somewhere. By default, it comes from what we may call the media class, which in turn is a part of the professional and managerial class. So, the BBC becomes in itself the institution that gives an imprimatur to certain kinds of ideas, beliefs and views. The whole production and presentation process will be subtly shaped by the belief that what is being done is not simply the delivery of a product but an educational act.

It is important to note that this is the case regardless of whether the motivation is broadly conservative or subversive. In the first case, the elevating process is that of articulating and sharing established knowledge and wisdom; in the second, it is to debunk and criticise that wisdom or the beliefs of a part of the public. In both cases, however, the intention is to improve and elevate the understanding of viewers and listeners by revealing what is believed to be objective truth in the first case and exposing what can objectively be described as error in the second. What is almost never subject to criticism is the internal received wisdom of the institution.

At the same time, the internal culture is not unchanging. What is clear from studies is that it lags behind changes of belief about certain matters in the worlds of politics and culture more generally. This redounds against both left and right at different times. Thus, in the 1970s and 1980s, the BBC was still supportive of the ideas of the post-war consensus, while today it still adheres to the ideas of the Blair years and, in many ways, the Thatcher and Major period. This enrages both conservatives of a certain kind and many leftists. As a conservative institution that adheres to a conventional wisdom, the BBC is typically slightly behind wider developments rather than leading them.

The problem of state funding

This is exacerbated by another structural feature of the BBC, which is the way its income source periodically puts it in a highly vulnerable position. Each time the licence fee comes up for renewal, the inevitable and institutionalised incentive is to tack towards the concerns of the government of the day. The political class in turn (or at least that part of it that is currently enjoying the emoluments of power) will take this opportunity to push the BBC in a direction that they find more pleasing. The result is a regular focus on issues that concern the political class rather than on, or to the exclusion of, issues that agitate many of the public, but which the politicians are broadly agreed upon. The result, again, is to consolidate a received wisdom: in this case, whatever political consensus there may be around certain issues. This effect is especially powerful when the political consensus coincides with the internal outlook of the organisation. Surprisingly, given the discussion around this topic, the BBC would enjoy much more independence if it were to move to a subscription-based funding model.

The result is that, while there will be debate and discussion around issues on which the political class is divided (but shaped and limited by the kinds of unexamined assumptions mentioned earlier), there will be either no discussion of issues on which there is a consensus, or the view will be overwhelmingly one-sided. Two examples of this are immigration, where, until very recently, a whole range of views were either dismissed or not given attention, and foreign and defence policy. Here, sceptical and critical views of those policy areas from both the radical left and dissident right are again either ignored or presented, not so subtly, as extreme and, therefore, not worth consideration.

The BBC, 'conventional wisdom' and the problem of nuanced views

This, in turn, raises another structural feature of the BBC that, in practice, leads to its output presenting a particular kind of conventional wisdom. This is the whole idea that in its news and current affairs coverage (but also in its business and financial reporting) it should aim for balance or neutrality in areas where there are clear debates. The obvious trap set by this approach is that of treating ludicrous or marginal ideas on the same footing as well-established and respectable ones. This is indeed a problem in the US, satirised in the spoof headline 'Shape of the world: views differ'. However, the BBC has definitely avoided that kind of blunder. Thinking about it, however, reveals the more profound problems raised by the whole idea of neutrality or impartiality in current affairs broadcasting. One difficulty is that of deciding which views count as marginal and which ones count as mainstream – sometimes this is clear, but often it is not. Even more troubling is the challenge of having a schema by which you can put different perspectives in a position relative to each other – if you cannot do this, then the whole idea of neutrality becomes moot.

This particular problem is made worse by an inherent feature of television as a medium (less so radio), which is that it has great difficulty dealing with debates in anything other than a binary opposition between two opposed sets of views. Multiple or overlapping views and positions, which is what we find in the real world, are very hard to physically present in a visual mode.[1] The

---

1 An example of this occurred when the editor was regularly invited to participate in BBC programmes following the Primark building collapse in Bangladesh. The IEA was frequently contacted to put forward in debate the view that companies had no moral or economic responsibilities towards their workers, and that this position was in the long-run best interests of the workers. The line that companies had certain moral responsibilities, but that there should not be government regulation in this area (in fact, there was already regulation, as it happens), was too nuanced. Assuming that the BBC found commentators, they would have been presented as

solution to the problem of knowing how to locate different views relative to each other, and therefore of how to strike a balance between them, is probably insoluble. The naïve view is that this can be done in two ways, either by splitting the difference between two views or by adopting a neutral standpoint that judges the competing positions from the outside.

Neither of these will work. The first produces an intellectual position that is usually incoherent and feeble. It will also lead to the position being pulled in one 'direction' or another on the arbitrary binary scale as the Overton Window shifts. The second has a basic philosophical problem: the supposed neutral or independent position cannot be an empty one; it has to be a substantive position of its own, because otherwise there is no basis on which to locate the competing views relative to each other. What happens in reality is the formation of a particular position, which will by default be the conventional wisdom at the time of either the internal culture or the political consensus, or both. That this is not a morally neutral position is shown by the language used to describe this revealed wisdom or centre of gravity: terms such as 'moderate' or 'respectable', as compared with 'extreme', 'unrespectable' or even (worst of all) 'populist'. A moment of thought will show the difficulty with this. Is it good to be 'moderately' rather than 'extremely' correct? Is the fact that an idea is accepted and widely shared proof of its validity? The answer appears to be yes when the ideas are held by some kinds of people, but not when they are held by others.

There are two further features that contribute to the institutional bias in favour of a kind of conventional wisdom, both of which were always present but have become more pronounced recently. The first is the deliberate severing of the BBC as a national institution from particular political or social groups or

---

one side believing in government regulation and moral restraint, and the other side believing in free markets, the absence of regulation and that companies and individuals have no moral obligations.

localities. Again, this means that, in reality, the organisation will come to establish procedures that privilege the perspective of a certain locality and group, which in this case is the metropolitan professional middle class (Scotland and Northern Ireland are a qualified exception to this). Another is the dependency of the BBC on news releases and information given to them by government and large organisations. This was always the case, but it has become much more marked with the advent of the 24-hour news cycle. The interesting reality, though, is that it has not affected commercial broadcasters in the same way. The reason, again, is the different incentives created by different funding models, and the different relationship with the state and the political class.

Conclusion

The reality is that the BBC does indeed have a bias, but this is not as simple as a bias to one side or the other of a one-dimensional political spectrum (indeed, it is thinking of political views in this way that is part of the problem). Rather, the composition of the BBC's staff and its internal culture, when combined with certain structural features of the BBC as an institution, mean that the processes of commissioning, production, delivery and presentation will always tend to produce an output with a particular kind of quality. There is a commitment to and focus on a received or conventional wisdom that is not the settled view of the population as a whole (to the very small extent that such a thing ever exists); it is not even the view of a real and definite 'establishment', but rather a way of thinking about politics, society and the world that is the inevitable result of the constraints imposed by the nature and mission of the BBC. It is also partly produced by the world-view of the kind of person who chooses to work at the BBC, combined with the consensual views of the political class, which has come to have an ever-closer connection to all the mass media.

This means that certain views are marginalised and either misrepresented or even ignored. It is not a straightforward matter of either left or right views being treated in this way. Rather, all views that are not in the conventional wisdom are slighted, even if they are widely held among the public. Examples from the right would be support for radical reform of the welfare system or the NHS; from the left, it could be the popularity of public ownership of utilities. In the extreme case of foreign policy and defence, there is actually very little scope for departure from a narrow range of positions – the sound and fury of arguments over details should not obscure this. Certain views are clearly represented as being uninformed or exotic, such as scepticism about man-made climate change, hostility to immigration or doubts about the benefits of formal education. Sometimes this judgement may be true, but to simply ignore and disregard a view is actually counterproductive if your aim is to inform.

In addition, there is an intensification of the structural tendency of the modern media to see political and intellectual divisions in binary terms. This leads to many perspectives being simply ignored or misrepresented. In the last 30 years, for example, it has become part of the conventional BBC view that opposition to the EU is definitively located on the right. This means that the continuing and at one time prominent socialist critique of the EU is simply not represented. On the other side, opposition to immigration is thought to be associated with other views conventionally placed on the right, so that left-wing opposition to labour migration is airbrushed out, despite being common among many Labour voters. At the same time, the strong support of most free-market advocates for freer immigration is ignored and glossed over. In other words, the very existence of certain kinds of combinations of views is simply ruled out, and they are not even considered, despite being perfectly coherent intellectually and widely held.

Changes in personnel and management will have some effect. However, as long as the BBC continues as a broadcaster with a peculiar status as a national institution, with a non-voluntary funding model, an explicit dedication to a particular conception of PSB and a statutory requirement to show balance, there will always be a bias in the very nature of the institution and its processes that, when combined with its staff profile, will produce a passionate commitment to a specific kind of style and world-view. This will be one that is seen by its adherents as simply obvious common sense, while a whole range of other positions do not find full expression and are neither articulated nor challenged.

As has been noted – in this chapter and the previous one – other forms of institutional framework will bring other biases. Given the fact that different institutions have different forms of bias, perhaps the best approach is to allow a process of competition to develop. This could involve the commercial and non-commercial production of broadcasting services, as long as they were funded on a voluntary basis. It is not the bias of the BBC that is the problem as such. The problem is the bias combined with the institution's market power (especially in news provision), its non-voluntary funding method and its closeness to the political process.

References

Chandler, D. and Munday, R. (eds) (2011) *Oxford Dictionary of Media and Communication*. Oxford University Press.

Chomsky, N. and Herman, E. S. (2002) *Manufacturing Consent: Political Economy of the Mass Media*. New York: Pantheon Books.

Denning, S. (2011) How do you change an organizational culture? *Forbes Magazine,* 23 July. www.forbes.com/sites/stevedenning/2011/07/23/how-do-you-change-an-organizational-culture/

Groseclose, T. (2012) *Left Turn: How Liberal Media Bias Distorts the American Mind*. New York: St Martin's Griffin.

Jones, O. (2014) It's the BBC's right wing bias that is the threat to democracy and journalism. *Guardian*, 17 March. www.theguardian.com/commentisfree/2014/mar/17/bbc-leftwing-bias-non-existent-myth.

Latham, O. (2013) Bias at the Beeb? A quantitative study of slant in BBC online reporting. Report, Centre for Policy Studies, London.

Milburn, A. (2014) Elitist Britain? Report, Social Mobility and Child Poverty Commission.

Perkin, H. (1990) *The Rise of Professional Society: England Since 1880*. London: Routledge.

Wahl-Jorgensen, K. et al. (2012) BBC breadth of opinion review. Report, Cardiff School of Journalism. http://downloads.bbc.co.uk/bbctrust/assets/files/pdf/our_work/breadth_opinion/content_analysis.pdf

5 PRIVATISING THE BBC[1]

Tim Congdon

Setting the scene

Time and technology wait for no organisation, no matter how revered. The next few months will see continuing lively public discussion over the future of the British Broadcasting Corporation, with the current Royal Charter due to run out at the end of 2016. The early talk was of an extension of the licence fee for a further decade to 2026, as well as of possible reductions in its value and certainly of freezing it in real terms. According to an ICM poll in the *Sunday Telegraph* on 3 November 2013, 70 per cent of voters believed that the licence fee should be abolished or cut. Another poll in July 2014, commissioned by the Whitehouse Consultancy of media analysts, found that 51 per cent of the public would support the idea of abolishing the licence fee and making the BBC fund itself (Ross 2014). On this basis, the British public was prepared for radical change in their nation's broadcasting.

The latest news (as of March 2016) is that no radical change is to be expected for at least another decade. Newspapers report that a deal has been done between George Osborne, the Chancellor of the Exchequer, and Lord Hall, the BBC's Director General. In the next licensing round, the BBC will have the bear the cost

---

1   This chapter is summarised from the ebook *Privatise the BBC* (2014), published by *Standpoint*, London, UK; it also uses material from articles published by the author in *Standpoint*. The IEA is grateful to *Standpoint* for permission to adapt and republish.

of free TV licences for those over 75 years old. (Previously, the government had fully compensated the BBC for the lost revenue.) The implied dent to the BBC's revenues, expected to reach £745 million in 2020/21, is substantial. It would amount to perhaps a fifth of the licence fee income it would otherwise have expected. Nevertheless, under the terms of the Osborne–Hall deal, the licence fee is to continue, at least for the decade to 2026. Indeed, the government is apparently concerned with protecting the 'tax base' on which the licence fee is levied, while its value is to rise with inflation. Significantly, it wants people who watch recorded programmes on the BBC's iPlayer to become liable for the licence fee, in contrast to the present situation in which the licence fee is payable only for the viewing of live productions.[2] However, other reports have it that the review process for the Royal Charter is continuing, with many aspects of the BBC's future funding and remit still undecided.[3]

Lord Patten, the former chairman of the BBC Trust (which has been scrapped), described the Osborne–Hall deal as 'quick and dirty', and 'awful'. Does the Osborne–Hall deal in fact define the government's ultimate position? If so, a fair verdict would be that the government has decided to ignore the case for a big and serious debate about the position of public sector broadcasting in a modern liberal democracy such as Britain. Arguably, a major opportunity would have been lost. In February 2014, Nick Ross, the former presenter of the BBC *Crimewatch* programme, warned that support for the BBC could 'fall off a cliff' if it did not prepare to ditch the licence fee. He claimed, paradoxically, that he was urging change because he treasured the BBC and wanted to secure its long-run future.[4]

---

2   Nick Higham, 'What will happen if BBC funds free licences?' 5 July 2015. 'News' section on www.bbc.co.uk.

3   Alexi Mostrous, 'Embattled BBC faces curbs on website and reality shows.' *Times*, 13 July 2015.

4   Nicholas Hellen, 'Star tells BBC to axe licence fee.' *Sunday Times*, 2 February 2014.

Ahead of the 2015 general election, no political party showed any inclination for root-and-branch reform. Most politicians involved in the drab and often bad-tempered debate about the structure of broadcasting tended to take for granted both the survival of the licence fee in some form and the BBC's status as a nationalised organisation. Prime Minister David Cameron is reported to have said that, while the BBC 'should be independent of government', it 'should not be privatised' (Scadding 2014: 294). It is worth noting also that proposals to privatise Channel 4, apparently supported by Conservative ministers in the 2010–15 coalition, were blocked by Vince Cable, their Liberal Democrat colleague, who was Secretary of State for Business, Innovation and Skills. Now that the Conservatives are in power and unconstrained by the Liberal Democrats, the privatisation of Channel 4 is again said to be under review.

The discussion in this chapter predates the Osborne–Hall deal and is developed almost as if it had not been done.[5] The main points are that the licence fee is now obsolete as well as unpopular, and that the ending of the licence fee would necessitate radical upheaval, both for the BBC and the structure of British broadcasting. With the licence fee scrapped and no alternative system of state funding put in its place, the BBC could not have remained in public ownership. The recommendation here is that it should then have been privatised, so that it could compete more freely with the global media giants that are now emerging. Without the licence fee, the BBC could flourish in the long run only with the revenue sources and management autonomy found in the large private sector media businesses of today. Over the decade from 2016, the Osborne–Hall deal appears to preclude a major upheaval of the sort recommended in these pages. However, the argument remains relevant over the longer term. (It is noteworthy that many

---

5 I presented the arguments that the licence fee should be scrapped and the BBC privatised in an article in the December 2013 issue of *Standpoint* magazine, 'Scrap the licence fee and privatise the BBC'.

of the media reports on the perhaps disjointed official response to the current licence review hint at its eventual abolition.[6])

The argument splits into two parts. One is concerned with the licence fee and the other with privatisation. Despite this separation, the two parts are logically related. In theory, licence fee money could be ladled out to a number of private, profit-seeking media companies 'on merit' by a committee of the great and the good, rather like the Arts Council. But, in practice, that would almost certainly result in huge and unacceptable controversy. Complaints would come both from international competitors, angered by the subsidies given to purely British entities, and from British-owned or British-managed companies rejected or snubbed by the committee. Meanwhile, not even in theory, let alone in any vaguely plausible real-world context, could the BBC be privatised if its dominant source of income were a state subsidy. The two proposals being made here are to be seen as inseparable twins.

The case for ending the licence fee

The case for ending the licence fee is presented by other authors in this book, and only aspects of it are developed in this chapter. In summary, the case has two main strands. Firstly, the advance of technology has destroyed the original and valid justification for the licence fee when it was introduced in 1946. Secondly, the method of collection is not just expensive and inefficient but has also become harmful in its wider effects.

Spectrum scarcity once made TV the classic 'public good'

In the early days of television in the 1940s, technology imposed tight constraints. The transmission of programmes 'over the air'

---

6   This is true, for example, of the Alexi Mostrous story in the *Times* on 13 July 2015, which mentioned an imminent green paper that would 'open the door for the eventual replacement of the licence fee, possibly after 2026'.

from land-based masts and towers was limited by a shortage of spectrum. Only one channel was readily feasible. Further, if programmes were broadcast free to air from the masts, any household with a TV set could watch. Pay-per-view and subscription for a particular channel were impossible.

Although payment could have been by advertising, the postwar Attlee government was hostile towards capitalism, consumerism and marketing jingles. The extent of the contemporary hostility to advertising is illustrated by *The Economic System in a Socialist State* by Robert Hall (1937). The author of this book believed that a society could be designed in which 'competitive advertising' could be abolished and only informative advertising would remain. He further thought that 'for this purpose a department of propaganda would be sufficient'. To later generations, who have read George Orwell's *1984* and *Animal Farm*, Hall's views may sound sinister, even outlandish. But he was not a maverick. On the contrary, he was appointed chief economic adviser to the British government in 1947 and stayed in that position until 1961, later becoming Lord Roberthall.

With payment by advertising proscribed, any broadcasting organisation depended on the state for funding. Of course, a state broadcaster could have been financed from taxation, but there were fears that a politically motivated administration might withhold money from a broadcaster critical of government actions. The BBC had therefore to be funded by a mechanism that enabled it to resist political pressure. The introduction in 1946 of the BBC licence fee for television was almost inevitable, given the political and technological setting. (It should be noted that a BBC licence fee for radio had set the precedent since 1926. The radio licence fee survived until 1973, when it was scrapped because the collection cost exceeded the amount raised.[7])

---

7   The problem of paying for the BBC's radio output is a nuisance for the analysis in this essay, as was pointed out by Anthony Fry in a letter in the January/February

Rigorous intellectual support was soon to emerge. Paul Samuelson (1954), the Nobel Prize–winning American economist, advanced the concept of 'public goods' or 'collective consumption goods' in a classic paper, which demonstrated that such goods had to be financed by a government levy of some kind and could not be left to the market. A public good was distinctive in being 'non-excludable' and 'non-rivalrous', meaning that individuals could not be effectively excluded from use of the good, and that use by one individual would not reduce its availability to others. Television fitted this model at the time.

In the decade or so from 1945, the BBC had extraordinary prestige, not least because of its reporting during World War II. Moreover, with the UK still accounting for over 5 per cent of world output, this state-owned monopoly was a vast broadcasting business by international standards. The BBC may not have been part of the British constitution, but it was undoubtedly a technological leader and a 'national champion'.

However, its special status was already being undermined. Spectrum scarcity – the original basis for monopoly – was being overcome by technical advances. In 1954, the Conservative government under Winston Churchill passed the Television Act, which allowed independent broadcasting financed by advertising to compete with the BBC. For the next 20 years, British broadcasting was a highly regulated duopoly of the BBC and the profit-hungry (and indeed very profitable) 'independent' television companies. Advertising continued to be demonised by left-wing commentators, and as long as advertising was the only other way to finance broadcasting, the licence fee was safe.

2014 issue of *Standpoint*, in response to the author's essay on the BBC in the December 2013 issue. If BBC radio is regarded as somehow sacrosanct and to be preserved for all time without a market-based funding mechanism (i.e. without advertising), a subvention from the government's tax revenue may be unavoidable.

Satellite-based broadcasting: a disruptive technology

By the 1980s, satellites with programme transmitting capability could be launched into space, promising a new world of satellite-based broadcasting. At first, two businesses were envisaged: Sky Television and British Satellite Broadcasting. (Sky Television, which had been created in 1978, was bought by Rupert Murdoch's News Corporation in 1983; see Horsman (1997: xi).) As both companies faced years of losses, they merged in 1990 to form BSkyB and make their plans more viable. The hope of the investors behind BSkyB was that viewers would pay for TV channels by subscription, usually on a monthly basis. Payment could now be related to the reception of a particular media output, with non-payers receiving nothing. That ended the problem of non-excludability that had been so important in the case for the licence fee 40 years earlier.

Murdoch and his associates had embarked on an ambitious long-term gamble, even if it was one that secured strong backing from the UK's big institutional investors. Ironically, BSkyB's investors became involved in this forward-looking and risky venture just as left-of-centre economists started to criticise the City of London for the alleged 'short-termism' of its time horizons and the supposed caution of its decision-taking.[8]

BSkyB initially made losses but, for the last decade, BSkyB has operated in the black, with annual profits reaching over £1 billion for the first time in 2011. As Figure 8 and Table 4 show, Murdoch and his backers brought about a huge change in how television was financed, produced and experienced by viewers. In November 2014 BSkyB acquired Sky Italia and a majority stake in Sky Deutschland, and the whole business is now known simply as Sky.

---

8   The usual reference here is to Hutton (1996).

Figure 8   The financing of British television today (£ billion revenues)

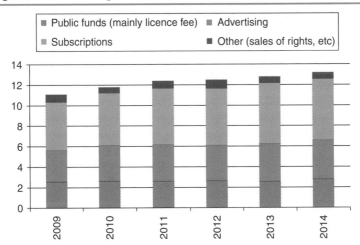

| ■ Public funds (mainly licence fee) | ■ Advertising |
| ■ Subscriptions | ■ Other (sales of rights, etc) |

Public funding for TV is less than the total licence fee, as this also pays for BBC radio and other services. Source: Ofcom (2015)

Is the BBC still dominant?

Rob Wilson, Conservative MP for Reading East, has used the word 'dominance' to characterise the BBC's position in news and current affairs broadcasting. Many analysts continue to see the BBC as dominant with an entrenched, almost unassailable position on the UK media scene. Perhaps even more attention grabbing than Wilson's observation was a statement by Harriet Harman, as the Shadow Deputy Prime Minister, at the Oxford Media Convention in 2013, that, 'The sheer scale of the BBC – the world's biggest broadcasting organisation – means that it is able to be, and is, a massive centre of gravity for our creative industries.'

The actual position is far more even-handed and complex, and far less comforting for the BBC's cheerleaders. The BBC is certainly not the world's biggest broadcasting organisation. As the growing unpopularity of the licence fee has constrained the

Table 4 **UK television industry metrics**

	2009	2010	2011	2012	2013	2014
Total TV industry revenue (£ billion)	11.1	11.8	12.4	12.5	12.8	13.2
Proportion of revenue generated by public funds (%)	23	22	21	21	20	21
Proportion of revenue generated by advertising (%)	28	30	29	28	29	29
Proportion of revenue generated by subscriptions (%)	42	43	44	44	46	45
Spend on originated output by five main networks (£ billion)	2.4	2.5	2.5	2.6	2.5	2.6
Digital TV take-up (% all households)	88	92	94	96	95	93
Percentage of DTV homes with pay satellite or cable	53	56	51	51	52	51
Minutes spent watching TV per day (per person aged 4+)	225	242	242	241	232	220
% share of the main five channels in all homes	58	56	54	52	51	51
Number of channels broadcasting in the UK	490	510	515	529	527	536

Source: Ofcom (2015)

BBC's revenues, TV advertising spend is now about the same size as the total money collected by the licence fee, and well above the portion of this money devoted to television. But the truly spectacular development of the last few years is that both total advertising spend and the licence fee money have been surpassed by BSkyB/Sky's subscription revenue. As BSkyB/Sky also picks up advertising revenue on its channels, its annual income is well above that of the BBC. In their last complete years – to 31 March 2015 for the BBC, and to 30 June 2015 for BSkyB/Sky – the BBC's income was £4.8 billion, of which £3.7 billion came from the licence fee, while BSkyB/Sky's was £9.9 billion. About 20 per cent of Sky's income came from its new European acquisitions, leaving its UK revenues – of which over 80 per cent came from

Figure 9   Is the BBC already an underdog?

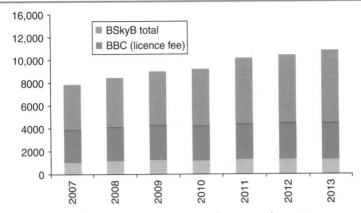

Total revenues (£ million). Source: Company annual reports and accounts.

subscriptions – at £7.8 billion. BSkyB/Sky has therefore overtaken the BBC in terms of market presence, and the BBC has ceased to be dominant, even in Britain itself (see Figure 9). The BBC does have an international arm, BBC Worldwide Ltd, with an avowedly commercial remit, but its sales are small compared with Time Warner, CBS, the Hearst Corporation, Murdoch's US-based firms including 21st Century Fox and Google. BBC Worldwide's revenues fell in the year to June 2015, even though the global media market continued to expand.

So, British broadcasting today is utterly different from the situation in 1946, when the licence fee began and the BBC enjoyed both massive global prestige and a monopoly position in its home market. On the face of it, three forms of payment are jostling with each other in the UK television market, namely the semi-tax licence fee money exclusively for the BBC, and advertising spend and subscription revenues for the other two types of participant. No participant is paramount, but in simple money terms Sky is now clearly in the lead. Just after World War II, UK broadcasting epitomised the Samuelson concept of a public good. For a long time, it was a regulated duopoly; for some years now, it has been a confusing oligopoly, with a mix of public and private ownership. Even if technology could somehow be stabilised for all time, the original case for the licence fee would have to be reformulated. The private sector businesses, led by Sky and ITV (much the largest of the remaining 'independent' companies), have carved out strong market positions. But they have done so only after taking great commercial risks and defying the blatant government subsidy given to the original state-owned industry leader.

But technology cannot be stabilised for all time. On the contrary, new payment structures and transmission arrangements are being conceived every few months. Such is the degree of flux at present that no one can give reliable long-term forecasts of the relative importance of different transmission and payment mechanisms. Sky, ITV and every other shareholder-owned media organisation in Britain faces intense competition, not only from other such organisations with a known commitment to a particular technology, but also from new organisations with distinctive and unexpected technologies. Transmission by means of cable has been available for a long time. But the most exciting of the new technologies is Internet or online broadcasting, and the most menacing of the new competitors are the telephone companies, which own the transmission capability (the copper wires or mobile frequencies), and Internet search engines such as Google.

Internet broadcasting: another disruptive technology

Telecommunications (telco) companies have a major inbuilt advantage with Internet broadcasting. Because they own the equipment that transmits Internet material, including streamed programming, they know the identities of the people and companies who benefit from that equipment. It is a relatively simple matter for them to add TV programming to the telephone package and to charge for the extra services. Plainly, when British Telecom, or indeed any telecommunications business, charges telephone users a subscription fee for broadcast material on top of the phone bill, it enters the subscription television business. It does so with no need to launch satellites or to lay extra cable underground. On 11 November 2013, British Telecom announced that it had bought the rights to screen 350 top football matches, in order that its telephone customers would watch them. The threat to BSkyB's business model was so obvious and disruptive that its share price fell almost 10 per cent within minutes of the announcement. Initially, British Telecom's return from its sports broadcasting came from a mixture of advertising revenue and a higher retention rate of its broadband customers. But now it would attack BSkyB/Sky's subscription model directly. A big competitive battle had started.

Not that BSkyB/Sky can have been surprised by British Telecom's invasion of its turf. For some years, it has wanted to persuade its TV subscription customers to choose BSkyB/Sky for telephone services as well. Both BSkyB/Sky and British Telecom are seeking to market not just broadcasting options but the so-called triple play of television, broadband and telephony.

However, a key point must be noticed. The Internet now has other, quite well-established ways of charging 'viewers'. All providers of content via the Internet, and not just British Telecom or another telco, can restrict access to their material by using widely available software. They can then allow viewing of the material only to people who pay. The Internet therefore becomes the vehicle not so much for broadcasting as for 'narrowcasting', understood as the channelling of specialised content to a well-defined and limited market. Technology is advancing so quickly that the narrowcast material no longer has to be pre-recorded; it can be live and sent out in real time. So, the big broadcasters are competing not only among themselves but also with a range of Internet-based rivals (bloggers selling advertising space, porn websites charging subscriptions, antique price comparison websites financed by auctioneers, hobby association websites with access included in a membership fee, classic film or music websites with a pay-per-download system and so on).

In short, 'broadcasting' may ultimately cease to exist as a distinct and definable category subject to specific and targeted regulation. Performances of all sorts are conveyed to customers by an assortment of technologies and financed by a number of payment arrangements. Nowadays, broadcasting as such is increasingly difficult to distinguish from interpersonal communication in general, and television and radio programmes are no longer a public good in the Samuelson sense. The original case for the licence fee is dead.

The BBC in the digital era

What are the implications of these unleashed market forces for the BBC? There have been proposals for some kind of digital enhancement to the licence fee to take account of the wide range of devices that can receive content.[9] However, this has become ridiculous for two main reasons.

Firstly, the miniaturisation associated with the digital revolution has made it possible to receive broadcasts over small devices, such as smartphones and tablets. Incredibly, the Blair government decided in the 2004 Communications Regulations that the licence fee should be imposed on households with computers that might be construed as televisions. Strictly speaking, the legal position today is that any device receiving a moving image in real time (in other words, which is not being transmitted as a

---

9 The most important of these was made in a 1999 committee, chaired by Gavyn Davies, on the BBC's financing in the digital era. The author debated the issues with Davies in an article, 'Does "new media" make the licence fee redundant?', in the April 2000 issue of *Prospect* magazine.

recorded version) must pay the licence fee. But no one has advocated that the licence fee be extended to smartphones and tablets, because officialdom would then have to check the reception ability of everyone's mobile phone and indeed landline connection. The notion of including phones in the licence fee 'tax base' is clearly untenable.

The BBC has itself acknowledged that the owners of devices using the iPlayer do not at present have to pay the licence fee, but the Osborne–Hall deal appears to imply that the BBC wants to enforce licence fee payment on recorded as well as live content. The iPlayer exemption was indeed the thin end of a wedge, and it was potentially a massive wedge that had been opened up. Surveys of viewing habits show that young people in particular watch BBC programmes on iPlayer on a 'time-shifted' basis. As a result, they have access to BBC content, but are not legally obliged to pay the licence fee. The larger message is that the distinctions between phones, computers and televisions have collapsed, and the notion of a definable tax base for the licence fee has broken down.

Secondly, broadcasting is being globalised. In the 1950s, old-fashioned transmission from masts and towers was specific to a particular locality; nowadays, satellites can be positioned for any country, and the Internet is in principle wholly international. In the new circumstances, broadcasts transmitted from one nation can be received in many nations, smudging the borders of the specific jurisdictions in which a tax or fee can be collected. Further, media giants targeting the global market are now emerging, and the concept of cross-border 'trade' in broadcasting has become a reality. In a world of this kind, broadcasting will increasingly be subject to the prohibitions on state subsidy found in the World Trade Organization's rules, and that means prohibitions on such relics of national broadcasting as the BBC licence fee.

These solvents of the licence fee arrangements exacerbate a long-term pre-existing problem. There is widespread evasion of payment of the licence fee. The UK has a law that says the non-payment of fines for licence fee evasion is a criminal offence, and – as long as that law is on the statute book – it must be enforced. However, it is costly to enforce, and a disproportionately large amount of magistrates' time is spent on licence fee cases. As a result of the controversy surrounding this, non-payment of fines for licence fee evasion now seems certain to be decriminalised in the next renewal of the BBC Charter.[10] The eventual result will be more non-payment and an erosion of BBC revenue. The BBC may react by trying to restrict access to its broadcasts by adopting the encryption technologies that have long enabled BSkyB to exclude non-payers from watching its output. If so, the BBC payment arrangements would, of course, be evolving in a market direction. As access would depend to an ever-greater extent on the encryption of content, the BBC would be moving towards a subscription model of payment!

Indeed, even a direct grant from government would generate significant cost savings. The cost of collecting taxes is much less than the cost of collecting the licence fee. Congdon (2014) suggests that treating PSB as part of public expenditure would lead to significant savings, perhaps as much as £200 million a year.

Common defences of state funding of broadcasting

National culture

It is often argued that private sector media companies are interested in profit, not in 'national culture', and certainly not in elite and highbrow culture. Let it be assumed for the sake of argument that the promotion of national culture, particularly in its highest forms, is of great benefit to society at large. It then follows that only a public sector broadcaster, or perhaps a private sector

---

10   Alisdair Glennie, 'MPs lift threat of jail for licence fee dodgers: BBC stripped of powers to bring criminal prosecutions after agreement by three main parties.' *Daily Mail*, 25 March 2014.

broadcaster in receipt of state subsidy, can override the profit motive and give weight to aesthetic, spiritual or cultural value in its programming decisions.

The weakness of this kind of argument is that it is paternalist. Its validity depends on the premise that an elite knows more about what is good for other people than those people do themselves. The risk is that paternalism turns into the suppression of choice and the denial of free expression. This is perhaps typified by the attitude of the first Director General of the BBC, John Reith, who stated in the early days of radio that 'few listeners know what they want, and very few want what they need' (Reith 1924: 34).

The notion of national culture is controversial, particularly in today's world of increasing multiculturalism and relativism of belief. If it is accepted that a nation has a distinctive culture, and that the defence of this culture is valid and important, a case might be made that a set of institutions is needed to conduct that defence.[11] When the BBC had a monopoly of the airwaves, there may have been some logic in seeing it in Reithian terms as one of those institutions. But opinion has shifted. The Peacock Report (1986) on the BBC upheld the principle of 'consumer sovereignty' and implicitly repudiated the Reithian legacy.

Meanwhile, appeals to the desirability of 'UK content', as if British creative input were in some way particularly deserving, are hollow. A test of the desirability of content already exists, and that is the test provided by the market. If the existence of the BBC causes British television to be 'the best in the world', as is sometimes said, then BBC Worldwide – which can sell BBC output on a profit-seeking basis across the globe – ought to be an immense success and a spectacularly profitable business. It is nothing of the sort. Yes, it has great content to sell to broadcasters in other countries and makes a profit. But, no, it is not to be put on a

---

11 For clarity, the author does believe that nations have distinctive 'cultures', and their defence is valid and important. Some of Roger Scruton's books (2007, 2014) are strong and challenging in this area.

pedestal as if it had far more high-quality content than any of its competitors. In truth, BBC Worldwide has struggled against much larger American rivals, such as HBO (Home Box Office Inc.), a subsidiary of Time Warner.[12]

Impartiality[13]

Another argument for state funding again reflects the BBC's past and indeed Britain's former position as the founder nation in the largest empire the world has ever seen. News and current affairs broadcasting is always likely to be biased to some degree, reflecting the political beliefs of programme sponsors and makers, and their nationality, ideology, religion and so on. Britain's historical achievements gave it a reputation for 'fair play' and as a defender of the 'level playing field'. The immediate post-1945 generation, in many countries and not just in Britain itself, saw the BBC as the champion of impartiality in a fractured and uncertain world. By contrast, profit-maximising commercial enterprises had no interest in maintaining impartiality in news and current affairs. A general argument for state funding was implied: the private sector paid no attention to the socially desirable objective of unbiased news reporting, and a broadcaster with state subsidy was required to fill the gap.[14]

---

12 The BBC does have an American arm. The BBC has negotiated a deal with a US cable TV network, AMC Networks, with AMC perhaps taking an equity stake in BBC America. (See 'Honourable deal can drive BBC's income from America.' *Times*, 1 August 2014.) AMC Networks was floated on Nasdaq in 2011 and, at the time of writing, had a market capitalisation of over $4 billion. It is a big business by UK standards, but it is small in the context of the American media market. (Time Warner's market capitalisation was over $75 billion at the same time.)

13 Editor's note: This issue is covered in other chapters in this book and is therefore only covered in brief here.

14 It is worth noting here that Churchill and Reith did not like each other. As Churchill was kept off air during the period he was warning about Nazi appeasement, concerns about bias at the BBC are not new. See Nick Robinson in an article in the *Daily Telegraph* on 4 October 2012, based on his then new book (Robinson 2012).

The need-for-impartiality rationale for state intervention may have had some plausibility in the first or perhaps even the second post-war generation. However, the complacency of post-war British society has been disturbed by such issues as immigration, the unity of the UK itself (with the 2014 Scottish referendum on independence) and the role of Islam in a constitutionally Christian society. The BBC has had difficulty positioning itself in a nation much less relaxed with itself than in the 1950s. As David Elstein noted in evidence to a House of Commons committee in January 2014, 'for probably 20 or 30 years the BBC have just been too nervous to deal with the subject [of immigration] directly'.[15]

Not only are some topics at risk of being ignored by the BBC, but accusations of bias are increasingly being levelled against its programming of contentious issues.

The usual criticism of BBC bias is not that it takes a well-defined Anglophile or Anglocentric line (in defence of the British nation, its sovereignty, religion and so on), but that it panders to political correctness. Even long-term BBC journalists have complained that its news coverage lacks bite and direction because of subservience to political correctness. Peter Sissons was a newscaster poached in 1989 from the independent television sector to front BBC programmes. To quote from his memoir *When One Door Closes* (Sissons 2011: 321),

> Bias is too blunt a word to describe the subtleties of the culture at TV Centre ... The better word for what pervades the BBC is mindset ... [A]t the core of the BBC, in its very DNA, is a mindset, a way of thinking, and an approach to ordering journalistic priorities, that is firmly of the left but not defined in any conventional political way. By far the most popular and widely read newspapers at the BBC are the *Guardian* and the *Independent*,

---

15 Oral evidence on 'The Future of the BBC', given to the Culture, Media and Sport Committee of the House of Commons on 14 January 2014, HC 949 (London: Stationery Office), p. 6. See also Ed West (2013).

and the numbers of these newspapers bought by the BBC seems to outnumber all the other newspapers that it provides.

In short, the BBC has ceased to be as open-minded, sceptical and neutral in its news and current affairs coverage as both its Royal Charter and its past reputation require. To recommend state subsidy for the promotion of impartiality assumes that the organisation receiving the subsidy is impartial. As the BBC has become vulnerable to bias, it is no longer a fitting recipient of the money. Moreover, recent academic research suggests that the best means of maintaining diversity in news and public affairs commentary, and so of letting people make up their own minds in a healthy liberal and democratic political culture, is competition in supply.[16]

Final remarks on the licence fee

The argument can now be pulled together. Licence fee money finances less than a quarter of the UK's television output; it is less important than advertising revenue and much smaller than the subscriptions collected by Sky. In the digital era, and particularly now that iPhones and Android devices have become commonplace, the licence fee no longer has a readily defined tax base and is increasingly impractical to collect. (This is true, despite the proposal in the Osborne–Hall deal to make BBC iPlayer viewers subject to the licence fee.) Moreover, in the run-up to its financing review the BBC is being criticised by many politicians for bias of one kind or another, and the licence fee does not command the popular support that it once did. Claims that 'British broadcasting is the best in the world' or that 'we must protect the BBC's impartiality' belong to a different era and do not withstand serious critical scrutiny.

---

16 The usual reference here is to Professor Matthew Gentzkow of the University of Chicago. See, for example, Gentzgow and Shapiro (2006, 2008).

The case for the privatisation of the BBC

Let us suppose that the licence fee is scrapped in due course, even if the latest indications are that this could be fifteen years away. Let us also assume that the demise of state funding of the BBC is accepted as necessary, to establish a level playing field between competitors in UK media. What, then, is to become of the BBC?

At present the licence fee represents about 70 per cent of the BBC's total income. Unless the BBC is to contract dramatically, that money will have to be replaced by a combination of sub-scription money, advertising revenue and other income-generating sources. Obviously, a transitional period in which the BBC receives a government grant is to be expected. Also obviously, that government grant would be unfair on Sky, ITV and other broadcasting businesses if it were to persist for any length of time. In the long run, all of the UK's broadcasting businesses as well as – let us not forget – all of its up-and-coming narrowcasting businesses must compete on the same terms. A state subsidy should not be paid to only one organisation.

Problems within the public sector

Could the BBC remain in public ownership? Could it be a publicly owned entity, subject to market pressures and required to generate a decent return on capital, and still somehow operate with the remit of a 'public service broadcaster'? In theory, that could be envisaged. The UK had several nationalised industries in the post-war period, and somehow they operated, produced goods and services, sold them, prepared reports and accounts and so on. But, over time, considerable disillusionment took hold. The 1979–97 Conservative governments privatised and deregulated most of them and also broke up the monopolies. It speaks volumes that the 1997–2010 Labour government did not reverse the privatisations.

Consider some of the problems of a BBC operating in the marketplace but remaining in the government's hands. Its nationalised status would make it answerable to the government of the day in a financial sense and to Parliament in more general terms. Its management would not have the same freedoms – to buy and sell other businesses, to hire and fire staff, to expand or contract in foreign jurisdictions – as its commercial rivals. As a nationalised industry, with an implicit state guarantee on its debts, the BBC would seem to have an advantage over its privately owned competitors in fundraising. On the face of it, it could pay a lower interest rate on its borrowings. In reality, one of the most unsatisfactory aspects of nationalisation in the 30 years to 1979 was that the industries had to obtain approval for capital expenditure decisions from the Treasury, leading to mistakes of both under-investment (in the case of the railway network) and over-investment (in nuclear power, where the true costs of decommissioning power stations only became apparent at privatisation). In the twenty-first century, any media business has to be able to take capital spending decisions quickly, flexibly and with clear management accountability. If it were publicly owned and answerable to the Treasury, it could not do that.

Tessa Jowell, the Labour politician, has proposed that the BBC should become a mutual company, like the Co-op.[17] The cooperative ideal may be viable in sectors with easily understood and standardised methods of production, such as food retailing and life insurance. But the media world is very different, with its stars and prima donnas, ratings wars and multiple delivery platforms,

17 To quote Ms Jowell, 'It is the public and the licence fee payers who should be in the driving seat. So the argument would be the BBC should indeed be owned by its licence fee payers. The BBC should become the country's biggest mutual.' The BBC Trust should be retained and its job would be to act as 'the cheerleader for the licence fee payer'. www.bbc.co.uk/news/uk-politics-24613224 (accessed 25 January 25 2016). Jowell's idea was endorsed by David Miliband, one of the contenders for the Labour Party leadership in 2010.

and unpredictable shifts in taste and technology. No example of a successful, mutually owned modern media business can be offered.[18] In any case, the Co-op's own recent travails should warn against too much daydreaming about the virtues of employee or customer ownership. The wider message cannot be escaped. In an industry such as television broadcasting, the notion of a state-owned business dependent on private revenue sources is almost as ludicrous as the licence fee is fast becoming. Once the licence fee has gone, and once any alternative system of government subsidisation is rejected as unfair to its commercial rivals, the privatisation of the BBC must follow.

The international dimension: maximising brand value

For the time being, the conclusions just drawn – that the licence fee is finished and that the BBC must be privatised – are not part of the established policy consensus. However, the main lines of the analysis are so straightforward that they must be familiar to the key decision-takers in Ofcom, the Department of Culture, Media and Sport, and the BBC itself. In a speech in the BBC Radio Theatre on 8 October 2013, the current director-general, Lord Hall, highlighted the corporation's move into the tablet era by praising the BBC's iPlayer, which was to be 'reinvented' in 2014 and made 'more bespoke', so that it would become 'the best in the world'. The BBC's news audience, then put at 250 million people, was to be doubled to 500 million by 2022. Hall applauded 'the UK's amazing array of arts and science institutions' and said that it would be the BBC's job 'to reach new audiences across the globe' for these institutions. The BBC was even apparently to move into corporate finance, as in future it would offer 'risk

---

18 The Scott Trust, with its ownership of the Guardian Media Group, comes to mind. Both its national newspapers, the *Guardian* and the *Observer*, are losing money, and they depend for their continued existence on a fund built up from the sale of more commercially focused businesses.

capital to the UK's creative industries'. In an earlier and also striking announcement at the end of August 2013, Hall had eulogised Google and California's Silicon Valley for their speed of decision-taking.

All of this may be excellent as interesting kite-flying, except that it cannot be reconciled with the BBC in receipt of a state subsidy and hamstrung by Royal Charter commitments as a public service broadcaster.[19] Most fundamentally, any loudly proclaimed ambition to be the 'best in the world' must be of interest, and perhaps concern, to unsubsidised broadcasters in other countries. The UK has a population of 63 million, but Hall's ambition is for the BBC's news audience to be 500 million, and for it to project the UK's 'arts and science institutions' to 'new audiences across the globe'. Yet the British government cannot pass laws to require licence fee payment from such an international audience, nor should the government subsidise such activities from taxation. Certainly the BBC should not use licence fee money to broadcast to the 99 per cent of the world's population that does not pay the licence fee. If the BBC wishes to expand services in this way, it will have to do so as a commercial entity.

In practice, once the licence fee has gone, the BBC would need the financial independence and management flexibility found in the private sector if it were to be a meaningful competitor. Indeed, an argument can be made that the BBC's long-run commercial opportunity is massive. The halo over the BBC may have diminished in brightness and clarity since the heyday of the late 1940s and 1950s, but the BBC brand remains unique. It may be hyperbole to say that the BBC is the top broadcasting brand in the English-speaking world, but it must still be true that the BBC

---

19 The author would also like to put on record his dismay that the Lord Hall of the October 2013 best-is-yet-to-come barnstorming and kite-flying is the same Lord Hall who agreed, in July 2015, to a shabby deal to cut BBC resources by a fifth in order to defend the indefensible licence fee.

is a top broadcasting brand in that world.[20] According to Andrew Scadding, head of public affairs for the BBC since 2003, a Populus survey of fourteen countries in October 2013 rated 'BBC One highest on quality out of 66 major TV channels', while BBC Two was in third place. Indeed, in his view, internationally 'the BBC's reputation is undiminished and [it] is a great ambassador for Britain abroad' (Scadding 2014: 295). The ending of the licence fee and the privatisation of the BBC would permit the BBC to compete, freely and aggressively, with other global media businesses. The value of the brand could be maximised.

Serving international markets: the benefits of economies of scale

The long-run business opportunity outside the UK must be far greater than that within the UK. Three points are to be emphasised in this context. Firstly, the UK's share of world output is falling. As people in other nations copy existing production technologies found in the UK and other relatively wealthy nations, the UK is likely to slide down the league tables of income per head. If the BBC's audience is restricted to the UK, its share of the global media market must diminish. It needs to look outside the UK if it is to achieve the growth that its brand makes possible.

Secondly, although Britain is no longer a great and powerful nation, its historical contribution to the rise of modern global civilisation in the nineteenth and twentieth centuries was disproportionate to its size. The notion of the 'Anglosphere' is sometimes advanced to include nations in which English is the national language and many aspects of the legal and cultural inheritance are shared. There is a wider concept of the Anglosphere that also encompasses nations in which the national language

---

20 Of course, the BBC also has brand strength outside the English-speaking world, but that is harder to exploit.

is not English, but in which English is the language of business, finance and high culture. This wider concept includes most of Africa and much of Asia, as well the Anglosphere narrowly understood.

Critically, the nations of South Asia (India, Pakistan, Bangladesh, Myanmar and Sri Lanka) belong to the wider Anglosphere. In these nations and Africa, population growth continues at well above the world-average rate. As a result, in the late twenty-first century, English will be either the first language or the main second language (and indeed the language of the professional elite) in countries with more than half of the world's population. The UK's own population will be a mere 1 per cent of these countries in total.

The BBC's head of public affairs boasts of the BBC's 'undiminished reputation' around the world. Excellent, but, if so, should the BBC confine its programming in the next few decades to UK-focused news, soap operas, quiz shows and the like? If we look ahead to the early twenty-second century, the global market opportunity for high-quality English-language-based broadcasting outside the UK could be 100 times that in the UK. As Sir Peter Bazalgette, the current chairman of the Arts Council and a former television producer, has said, 'the government is discovering that there's this thing called the creative sector, growing twice as fast as the economy in general and increasing employment much faster than that. It exports and also burnishes the reputation (or "brand" in marketing speak) of Britain around the world.'[21]

Thirdly, films, videos and audio recordings are characterised by increasing returns to scale.[22] In the extreme, an extra viewer

21 Peter Bazalgette, 'Ideas for sale.' 'Exporting for Growth' supplement to the *Spectator*, 12 July 2014.

22 See Gavyn Davies (2004) for an excellent statement of the argument that the broadcasting market is characterised by market failure, with an emphasis on p. 22 on the effect of increasing returns to scale on market structure. The theme has remained in Davies' contributions to the debate on UK broadcasting, including his evidence

over the Internet can see another programme at virtually zero resource cost and a negligible addition to the phone bill, but the broadcaster can charge on a pay-per-view or subscription basis, and perhaps introduce paid-for advertising content on the screen. The cost to the viewer (of the pay-per-view) may be as little as $5 per hour, but for the broadcaster both that $5 and perhaps $1 of advertising revenue are virtually pure profit.

Global audiences of a billion are now feasible in technological terms. Meanwhile, the political and demographic trends of today imply that English will undoubtedly be the language of most programmes with such audiences. Obviously, with each viewer in that billion responsible for, say, $6-an-hour profit for the media business transmitting the programme, the business achieves a profit of $6 billion in one hour. That is roughly equal to the BBC's annual licence fee income at present. If the last few sentences sound like fantasy, it should be pointed out that the strategists at the often reviled 'Murdoch empire' are already thinking in these terms.[23] As noted above, in the autumn of 2014, BSkyB acquired 100 per cent of Sky Italia and 57.4 per cent of Sky Deutschland from 21st Century Fox. The explicit aim was to sell substantially the same content to a larger market. In other words, the objective was to take advantage of the increasing returns to scale found in the media industry. Here, it was being promoted in the European setting, but over time the relevant market context will be global.

---

to parliamentary committees. For a technical counter-argument, with much the same themes as the current publication, see Armstrong (2005). Davies continues to argue for an increase in the licence fee in real terms, although his position is now an outlier in the public debate. See the report in the *Daily Telegraph* on 23 January 2013, 'Licence fee "may need to rise" says former chairman Gavyn Davies'.

23 In oral evidence to the House of Commons' Culture, Media and Sport Committee on 11 February 2014, Greg Dyke, chairman of the BBC Board of Governors from 2001 to 2004, described 'the Murdoch organisation' as 'our long-term enemies ... or certainly opponents of the BBC'. For another example, see Peter Jay, 'Good riddance to Murdoch: one of the two things I loathe most,' in the August 2011 issue of the London-based *Prospect* magazine.

Perhaps even more emphatic an example of the larger argument is provided by the astonishing commercial success of Google, which collects advertising revenues as a by-product of its search engine capability. These revenues, which are global in source, are now similar in one month to the BBC's licence fee revenue in a year. The concept of Google would have been science fiction when the BBC licence fee was first introduced.

A possible alternative approach: a smaller BBC?

An alternative approach involves a commitment to PSB, as if this were a desirable end in its own right, but with a smaller BBC.

Suppose that all the reasons for abolishing the licence fee and the state financing of one broadcasting organisation, and indeed for abolishing the state financing of broadcasting in its entirety, are set out. Suppose that they are found convincing. The enthusiasts for PSB are put in a quandary. In their view, public sector broadcasting is a good thing. But it is not an absolute good, while the BBC's increasing political unpopularity and the evils of the licence fee mean that something has to change. What are the enthusiasts for PSB to believe in and advocate? One response is to compromise and plead that 'the time is not ripe'. Instead of abolishing the licence fee and ending state subsidy, the supporter of public sector broadcasting might suggest that the value of the licence fee should be kept constant in real terms or reduced only slightly. Furthermore, the BBC should cease trying to be both a producer of popular programmes and a champion of higher things such as 'culture'. The implied recommendation is pragmatic: it should drop a certain amount of the popular programming and stick to 'what it is best at'. In other words, a smaller BBC would be a better BBC. Policymakers should trim and compromise; they should avoid radical upheaval.

A reduction in the BBC licence fee, combined with some shedding of its popular programming ambitions, may well be the outcome of the current review of the BBC's role. (This does indeed seem to be the intended import of the Osborne–Hall deal, although it is not clear that the Osborne–Hall deal is the government's final verdict.) Radical change (licence fee abolition and privatisation), with the aim of promoting a big global-market BBC in the decades to come, will be rejected. Instead, decent and well-intentioned supposedly 'pro-BBC' people will recommend that the licence fee and the BBC should stay much as they are today, but they should be a little bit smaller and more modest.

They will recommend a smaller BBC, even though the impact of a fall in licence fee revenue on staff morale and programme quality would be problematic at best. Ambitious and talented people will not want to pursue careers in an organisation that is condemned, apparently by those who wish it well, to never-ending relative decline. The best and brightest in British broadcasting will instead choose to work in the revenue and profit-seeking private sector, in companies such as Sky and ITV, and in the Internet start-ups that are now proliferating.

Britain has much to gain in the twenty-first century from having a big BBC that establishes a strong position in the burgeoning world market for media products. No management guru has applauded compromise and equivocation as the best ways of reaching decisions, but that is invariably how UK official committees proceed. On this basis, a smaller BBC would be a worse BBC.

As we have seen, on becoming the director-general of the BBC in April 2013, Tony Hall said that 'the BBC's best years are yet to come'. A few months later, in the set-piece speech quoted earlier, he urged the merits of the BBC's iPlayer and declared that it should aim to be 'the best in the world'. Hall's message in April 2013 was that he wanted the BBC to look forward to growth and prosperity, and to be a global competitor. He favoured a big and expanding BBC, not a small and contracting one.

But Hall has also said that he supports PSB and, implicitly, the licence fee or state subsidy of some form. Yet, the BBC can participate in global markets as a meaningful competitor only if it is privately owned and profit maximising. It cannot be privately owned and profit maximising, and it cannot be big and expanding, if it is subject by an overriding legislative constraint to provide PSB to the licence fee payers, or to the taxpayers, of one small nation. Hall has proclaimed that the BBC must be 'the best in the world', just as it was in the late 1940s and 1950s. But is the money for the reinvented and bespoke iPlayer, and for the half-billion-strong global news audience, to come from advertising, from subscription, from pay-per-view or from another new and magical source so far wholly unknown to analysts of the broadcasting sector? Is it not obvious that the BBC cannot be both a significant player in global broadcasting and a state-owned organisation benefiting from public subsidy?

Global ambitions cannot be financed by licence fee money. Furthermore, the BBC cannot simultaneously receive a state subsidy heading towards £4 billion and direct hundreds of millions of 'risk capital' towards creative-industry entrepreneurs. Either the BBC is a profit-seeking, privately owned, risk-taking and slim-line enterprise, or it is a state-subsidised, state-owned, publicly accountable and rather bureaucratic behemoth. It cannot be both. At present, it is state-subsidised, state-owned, publicly accountable and rather bureaucratic.

The regulatory ecology of modern broadcasting is not yet settled. That is particularly true of broadcasting that crosses borders and caters for the global marketplace rather than a large number of separate national markets. But the next twenty or so years are likely to see international agreement on the terms of cross-border competition as well as the legal and regulatory structures that will enable it. Global media giants, including Google and the world's largest telephone companies, are already working out the strategies in which they can prosper as the changes unfold. A small BBC, a BBC fixated on the UK's own limited market and constrained by public service

Figure 10 **Global TV industry revenues by source (£ billion)**

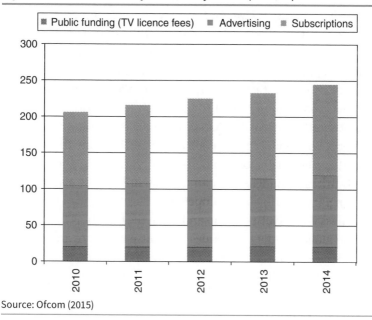

Source: Ofcom (2015)

commitments of one sort or another, cannot be a meaningful long-run competitor in world broadcasting. Ofcom has estimated that, globally, subscription revenues are now running at six times the value of public funding for broadcasting and continue to grow strongly while public funding remains static (see Figure 10). The implied message is straightforward: organisations dependent on public funding will stagnate and suffer relative decline. In an interview with the *Telegraph* on 19 March 2016, Tony Hall defended the BBC's role in drama ('in the BBC's lifeblood'), but admitted that the BBC cannot hope to match the spending of an organisation like Netflix, which plans to spend $5 billion (£3.5 billion) on original commissions in 2016. In Hall's words, 'We can't win against a Netflix or an Amazon, because their budgets are so much bigger...We have to think differently. We have to think like Drake's ships [against the Spanish Armada]. We've got to think lighter, simpler.'

It was established earlier that the BBC does not nowadays dominate broadcasting in Britain, and it certainly does not dominate broadcasting internationally. Once privatised and without artificial state support, the BBC would be a challenged organisation. It might need to seek cash to improve its content and strengthen its technology.[24] It might even eventually want to merge with a large telco, such as British Telecom or Vodafone, or perhaps even a telco with non-British ownership and management. British broadcasting can flourish only if it is also open to foreign participation and competition.

Unless it is privatised soon and given the freedoms to compete, the big global media companies will outmanoeuvre and outgun the BBC. As a lumbering bureaucracy in public ownership and dependent on state subsidy, the BBC will go the same way in the twenty-first century as British Leyland and British Shipbuilders did in the twentieth.

References

Armstrong, M. (2005) Public service broadcasting. *Fiscal Studies* 26(3): 281–99.

Davies, G. (2004) The BBC and public value. Essay, Social Market Foundation, London.

Gentzgow, M. and Shapiro, J. (2006) What drives media slant? Evidence from US daily newspapers. Working Paper 12707, National Bureau of Economic Research.

Gentzgow, M. and Shapiro, J. (2008) Competition and truth in the market for news. *Journal of Economic Perspectives* 22(2): 133–54.

---

24 Some cash might, of course, be raised if and when the BBC were floated on the stock market. Alternatively, shares might be distributed to the general public as part of a package that included subscription to BBC programmes and channels.

Hall, R. (1937) *The Economic System in a Socialist State*. London: Pickering & Chatto.

Horsman, M. (1997) *Sky High: The Inside Story of BSkyB*. London: Orion Business Books.

Hutton, W. (1996) *The State We're In*. London: Vintage Books.

Ofcom (2015) The communications market 2015. Report, Ofcom. http://stakeholders.ofcom.org.uk/binaries/research/cmr/cmr15/UK_2.pdf (downloaded 25 January 2016).

Peacock Report (1986) *Report of the Committee on Financing the BBC: Cmnd 9824*. London: Her Majesty's Stationery Office.

Reith, J. (1924) *Broadcast over Britain*. London: Hodder and Stoughton.

Robinson, N. (2012) *Live from Downing Street*. London: Bantam.

Ross, T. (2014) Public want BBC licence fee scrapped. *Sunday Telegraph*, 6 July.

Samuelson, P. A. (1954) The pure theory of public expenditure. *Review of Economics and Statistics* 36(4): 387–89.

Scadding, A. (2014) The best is yet to come. In *Is the BBC in Crisis?* (ed. J. Mair, R. Tait and R. L . Keeble). Bury St Edmunds: Abramis.

Scruton, R. (2007) *Culture Counts*. New York: Encounter Books.

Scruton, R. (2014) *The Soul of the World*. Princeton University Press.

Sissons, P. (2011) *When One Door Closes*. London: Biteback.

West, E. (2013) Groupthink: can we trust the BBC on immigration? Report, New Culture Forum, London.

ABOUT THE IEA

The Institute is a research and educational charity (No. CC 235 351), limited by guarantee. Its mission is to improve understanding of the fundamental institutions of a free society by analysing and expounding the role of markets in solving economic and social problems.

The IEA achieves its mission by:

- a high-quality publishing programme
- conferences, seminars, lectures and other events
- outreach to school and college students
- brokering media introductions and appearances

The IEA, which was established in 1955 by the late Sir Antony Fisher, is an educational charity, not a political organisation. It is independent of any political party or group and does not carry on activities intended to affect support for any political party or candidate in any election or referendum, or at any other time. It is financed by sales of publications, conference fees and voluntary donations.

In addition to its main series of publications the IEA also publishes a quarterly journal, *Economic Affairs*.

The IEA is aided in its work by a distinguished international Academic Advisory Council and an eminent panel of Honorary Fellows. Together with other academics, they review prospective IEA publications, their comments being passed on anonymously to authors. All IEA papers are therefore subject to the same rigorous independent refereeing process as used by leading academic journals.

IEA publications enjoy widespread classroom use and course adoptions in schools and universities. They are also sold throughout the world and often translated/reprinted.

Since 1974 the IEA has helped to create a worldwide network of 100 similar institutions in over 70 countries. They are all independent but share the IEA's mission.

Views expressed in the IEA's publications are those of the authors, not those of the Institute (which has no corporate view), its Managing Trustees, Academic Advisory Council members or senior staff.

Members of the Institute's Academic Advisory Council, Honorary Fellows, Trustees and Staff are listed on the following page.

The Institute gratefully acknowledges financial support for its publications programme and other work from a generous benefaction by the late Professor Ronald Coase.

Other books recently published by the IEA include:

The Profit Motive in Education – Continuing the Revolution
Edited by James B. Stanfield
Readings 65; ISBN 978-0-255-36646-5; £12.50

Which Road Ahead – Government or Market?
Oliver Knipping & Richard Wellings
Hobart Paper 171; ISBN 978-0-255-36619-9; £10.00

The Future of the Commons – Beyond Market Failure and Government Regulation
Elinor Ostrom et al.
Occasional Paper 148; ISBN 978-0-255-36653-3; £10.00

Redefining the Poverty Debate – Why a War on Markets Is No Substitute for a War on Poverty
Kristian Niemietz
Research Monograph 67; ISBN 978-0-255-36652-6; £12.50

The Euro – the Beginning, the Middle … and the End?
Edited by Philip Booth
Hobart Paperback 39; ISBN 978-0-255-36680-9; £12.50

The Shadow Economy
Friedrich Schneider & Colin C. Williams
Hobart Paper 172; ISBN 978-0-255-36674-8; £12.50

Quack Policy – Abusing Science in the Cause of Paternalism
Jamie Whyte
Hobart Paper 173; ISBN 978-0-255-36673-1; £10.00

Foundations of a Free Society
Eamonn Butler
Occasional Paper 149; ISBN 978-0-255-36687-8; £12.50

The Government Debt Iceberg
Jagadeesh Gokhale
Research Monograph 68; ISBN 978-0-255-36666-3; £10.00

A U-Turn on the Road to Serfdom
Grover Norquist
Occasional Paper 150; ISBN 978-0-255-36686-1; £10.00

New Private Monies – A Bit-Part Player?
Kevin Dowd
Hobart Paper 174; ISBN 978-0-255-36694-6; £10.00

From Crisis to Confidence – Macroeconomics after the Crash
Roger Koppl
Hobart Paper 175; ISBN 978-0-255-36693-9; £12.50

Other IEA publications

Comprehensive information on other publications and the wider work of the IEA can be found at www.iea.org.uk. To order any publication please see below.

Personal customers

Orders from personal customers should be directed to the IEA:

Clare Rusbridge
IEA
2 Lord North Street
FREEPOST LON10168
London SW1P 3YZ
Tel: 020 7799 8907. Fax: 020 7799 2137
Email: sales@iea.org.uk

Trade customers

All orders from the book trade should be directed to the IEA's distributor:

NBN International (IEA Orders)
Orders Dept.
NBN International
10 Thornbury Road
Plymouth PL6 7PP
Tel: 01752 202301, Fax: 01752 202333
Email: orders@nbninternational.com

IEA subscriptions

The IEA also offers a subscription service to its publications. For a single annual payment (currently £42.00 in the UK), subscribers receive every monograph the IEA publishes. For more information please contact:

Clare Rusbridge
Subscriptions
IEA
2 Lord North Street
FREEPOST LON10168
London SW1P 3YZ
Tel: 020 7799 8907, Fax: 020 7799 2137
Email: crusbridge@iea.org.uk